This is a book about what matters in the church, not about what is trendy, weighty, or popular. *Preaching the Cross* is a book about what endures, not what is momentarily successful. It is about what God intends for the church—that we preach his Word with its center in the person and work of Christ—and it is about what the church needs most to hear. These essays are written with wisdom, winsomeness, practicality, and biblical fidelity.

> —DAVID F. WELLS, Andrew Mutch Distinguished Professor
> of Historical and Systematic Theology,
> Gordon-Conwell Theological Seminary

This book on preaching the cross is written by the best of men who know the grace of the crucified Christ and serve in the power of his resurrection. It is a call for other ministers of the gospel to faithfully proclaim the message of the cross and the empty tomb. It is also an invitation to share in the fellowship of godly pastors who stand together for Jesus in a world that needs the gospel.

> —PHILIP G. RYKEN, Senior Minister,
> Tenth Presbyterian Church

TOGETHER FOR THE GOSPEL

PREACHING THE CROSS

**Mark Dever, J. Ligon Duncan III,
R. Albert Mohler Jr., C. J. Mahaney**
Contributions by John MacArthur, John Piper, R. C. Sproul

CROSSWAY BOOKS
WHEATON, ILLINOIS

Cover design: Josh Dennis

Cover photo: iStock

First printing 2007

Printed in the United States of America

Unless otherwise indicated, Scripture quotations are from *The Holy Bible, English Standard Version,*® copyright © 2001 by Crossway Bibles, a publishing ministry of Good News Publishers. Used by permission. All rights reserved.

Scripture quotations marked KJV are from the *King James Version* of the Bible.

Scripture quotations marked NASB are from *The New American Standard Bible.*® Copyright © The Lockman Foundation 1960, 1962, 1963, 1968, 1971, 1972, 1973, 1975, 1977, 1995. Used by permission.

Scripture references marked NIV are from *The Holy Bible: New International Version.*® Copyright © 1973, 1978, 1984 by International Bible Society. Used by permission of Zondervan Publishing House. All rights reserved.

The "NIV" and "New International Version" trademarks are registered in the United States Patent and Trademark Office by International Bible Society. Use of either trademark requires the permission of International Bible Society.

Scripture references marked NKJV are from *The New King James Version.* Copyright © 1982, Thomas Nelson, Inc. Used by permission.

All emphases in Scripture quotations have been added by the author.

Library of Congress Cataloging-in-Publication Data

Preaching the Cross / Mark Dever . . . [et al.].

    p. cm.

Includes bibliographical references.

    ISBN 13: 978-1-58134-828-6 (hc : alk. paper)

    1. Preaching—Congresses. 2. Bible—Homiletical use—Congresses. 3. Pastoral theology—Congresses. I. Dever, Mark. II. Title.

BV4211.3.P735   2007

251—dc22   2006035949

LB		16	15	14	13	12	11	10	09	08
13	12	11	10	9	8	7	6	5	4	3

For the next generation
of preachers of the cross

CONTENTS

INTRODUCTION

H as it ever occurred to you that one hundred pianos all tuned
to the same fork are automatically tuned to each other? They
are of one accord by being tuned, not to each other, but to another
standard to which each one must individually bow. So one hundred
worshippers meeting together, each one looking away to Christ, are
in heart nearer to each other than they could possibly be were
they to become 'unity' conscious and turn their eyes away from
God to strive for closer fellowship."[1] —A. W. Tozer

> *Dear Brothers,*
>   *We welcome you. We have come together for the gospel,*
> *which is the desire and passion for our lives and ministries.*
> *We pray that your life's passion and calling are the gospel*
> *of Jesus Christ.*

So began our letter of welcome to the pastors attending the 2006
Together for the Gospel conference. One of the unusual features
of the conference was the public conversations between Ligon,
C. J., Al, and me (Mark). We conversed onstage, not because our
comments are necessarily profound but because the fellowship
between us is so warm. Then and now we want to demonstrate to
you, our fellow pastors, that we care about our individual ministries only as far as they are a reflection of our caring about the

---

[1] Quoted by R. Kent Hughes in *Worship by the Book*, ed. D. A. Carson, (Grand Rapids, MI: Zondervan, 2002), 151. [Cited from A. W. Tozer's *Pursuit of God*, 97.]

gospel. When we have the gospel in common, we have all that's essential for time and eternity (though still maybe not enough to join each other's churches! But that's another conversation, and maybe one we'll have in front of you some day.).

The four of us richly benefit from our interactions with one another. I am still trying to learn graciousness at the feet of that most gracious of men, Lig Duncan, and I know that Lig would say that he has been encouraged and instructed in everything from complementarianism to humility by C. J. Mahaney. I know also that C. J. sees Al Mohler as about the most heroic man he's ever met, and I think Al likes the way that I try to encourage others to befriend his scary self! I could go on, but you get the idea.

Additionally, the four of us have learned much over the years from the special men who spoke along with us at the conference and whose talks appear in the chapters following. R. C. Sproul has had an influence for a generation now that is unusually wide and deep in upholding the gospel of the Lord Jesus Christ. John Piper has been used by God to bring freshness to our understanding of God's sovereign goodness. And John MacArthur has been providing a model of faithfulness in biblical preaching since before most of us were even converted.

Every once in a while God uses a conference such as this in a strategic way to put new heart in his under-shepherds and so bless his people. We prayed that this would be such a conference, that through it God would tune our hearts and minds to him as we thought and talked together about preaching the gospel of the Lord Jesus Christ. We prayed that those who attended would know great blessing from it.

Now, long after the conclusion of that event, we want to give thanks to God for the encouragement many did indeed experience as a result of that gathering and for the instruction given and friendships made there. In introducing this volume, which is comprised of the conference addresses, I want to say a little bit more about the history of the conference, the "heroes" we invited to join us, and the hopes that we had for the conference attendees—and for you as you prepare to read these messages.

A Conference with History

The conference is rooted in the unusual friendship that the four of us enjoy. We're all about the same age (except for C. J., who is old enough to be our dad, but he has exceptional athletic ability!). I met these extraordinary men one by one. Al Mohler and I became friends more than twenty years ago when we were students at The Southern Baptist Theological Seminary. The depth and range of Al's knowledge was apparent from our first conversation. I remember telling David Wells not long afterward that he would hear about this young friend of mine one day! The intensity with which Al lives was evidenced in the number of times he rang my phone after midnight, asking, "Mark, are you up?" (Given the hour, the question begged for a smart response, but I don't think I ever gave one.)

In subsequent years, I moved away to England. On visits to various cathedrals I obtained two copies of accompanying literature—one set for me, another for Al. He was my most faithful correspondent and encouraged me throughout my Ph.D program, and he has continued to do so since I took up the pastorate in Washington DC, even as his own life has become so busy.

Great Britain is where Lig Duncan came into my story. One of his friends from Covenant Seminary, Randy, was doing his Ph.D at Cambridge while I was studying there as well, and my family often shared meals with Randy's family. One day Randy asked me if I happened to know a friend of his, Lig, who had preached at their Presbyterian church on Sunday. He suggested we would get along well, so he got Lig on the phone, and we wound up talking for quite a while. I subsequently visited him several times up in Edinburgh, and he visited Connie and me down in Cambridge. Even then Lig was remarkably informed about everything that has happened from the patristic era (his field of doctoral study) up through the day before yesterday—all before the days of the Internet!

Lig became a close friend as we talked and prayed together about so many things, not least of which were some large life decisions that we faced simultaneously. Lig returned to the United States where he met Al, who was speaking at an RTS faculty retreat. Their friendship too has since grown; Al and Lig have provided help and encouragement to each other over the years. Lig is unflagging in graciousness toward others—even Baptists!

And then there's C. J., whom Don Whitney advised me to meet when I moved to the DC area. I neglected to do so, but in God's providence Aaron Menikoff and I had plans to visit a church member living in a retirement home near Covenant Life Church where C. J. was pastor. Aaron wanted to stop at the church and get a copy of Josh Harris's book *I Kissed Dating Goodbye* (Josh was associate pastor there at the time). I initially refused but then changed my mind and decided to try to find C. J. and introduce myself. But C. J. was in a meeting, so I simply left my card. He phoned me a few days later, and we had the first of what has become a series of enjoyable, edifying, challenging, intense lunches. C. J. has been a unique counselor to me since that first day, telling me what to do, with love, sensitivity, wisdom, and confidence. C. J. soon met Lig Duncan through their mutual involvement in the Council on Biblical Manhood and Womanhood. They got on warmly and have been a great encouragement to each other.

Sometime later I traveled to join C. J. at a New Attitude conference in Louisville. We met up with Al, and the three of us had a great time talking. We all commented on the fact that we missed having Ligon there, so we arranged to try to have him join us at our next meeting. And he did! This was the first of many such gatherings.

It was at one of those meetings that, during our typically long, enjoyable, question-then-anecdote-then-straight-into-argument-and-then-into-passionate-agreement conversations, one of us (I think it was Al, but we all were making the same kind of noises) remarked on the edifying nature of our conversations, and we all expressed a desire for pastors to experience this same sort of fellowship. As we talked, we came up with the idea of holding a conference at which the four of us would speak and afterward sit around and talk about the talks in front of our audience. (We talk about the talks late at night anyway, whenever we find ourselves together at a conference, although we do it without the audience!) We weren't sure what kind of audience we would get for our event, but we knew that we'd enjoy it no matter who came; any benefit accruing to others would be a bonus.

We thought that interest in the conference might be generated in part because of our differences, which actually serve to highlight our agreements. Al and I might have a few disagreements, but few, if any, are substantial. However, Ligon is a Presbyterian (though he and Al are both accused from time to time in their respective circles of being advocates for the other's denomination). We thought it would be interesting to see how much the three of us, from somewhat different ecclesiologies, stand together on the gospel and the various challenges confronting it today, but throw C. J. into the mix and the conference would really become interesting! I could keep going, but you get the idea.

We were sold. Matt Schmucker of 9Marks led with quiet and relentless faithfulness in the organization and administration of the conference with remarkable help (an understatement!) from Paul Medler and the Sovereign Grace Ministries conference team.

As I said the first night of the conference, we came together for the gospel. We wanted to encourage pastors, who are subjected to many shifting winds of doctrine and practice. Of course, the four of us didn't agree on what to wear or what kind of pulpit to use, and we barely came to agreement on the music, since our musical expression varies greatly. Some of us respond to sermons with applause while the others say *amen* (and even that we pronounce differently!). But we didn't come together to showcase our differences. We came together to highlight what we agree on—we came together for the gospel. My message lays out the nature of the calling of the true Christian minister, which is preaching God's Word. Lig Duncan's address is a masterful summation of how Christian ministers are to preach from the Old Testament. Al Mohler does a wonderful job of explaining how our preaching is to be culturally appropriate and penetratingly applied. And C. J.'s message is a reminder that the cross is to appear not just in our preaching but in our lives.

Our hopes were deeply blessed. Local ministers came, along with others from as far away as India and Australia. The attendees ranged from young seminary students to pastors who have shepherded a congregation for decades. They were Baptist and non-denominational, charismatic and Presbyterian, Anglican and Methodist—pastors who tend to disagree on any number of matters. But we came together for the gospel.

A Conference with Heroes

But this volume has seven authors, not just four. We agreed that we would enlarge the conference—its enjoyment for us, its attraction and usefulness to others—if we could include some of our own preaching heroes. We quickly agreed on three we wanted to invite, and they graciously agreed to come.

John MacArthur came to share with us his experience of preaching the cross, which he has been doing almost as long as many of us have been alive. We thought his example of long faithfulness would encourage the young ministers attending, who are, no doubt, fearful from many stories of shipwrecked ministries that loom large because they've come to realize how easy it is to steer off course. We thought John's ministry would bring glory to

God and comfort to them. And it did. And I think it will to you too as you look at his story, which is recounted in the last chapter of this volume.

R. C. Sproul also agreed to come. We could think of no one who draws a clearer distinction on where the gospel stands or falls. For decades R. C. has articulated that salvation comes not from our cooperating with God but from God's righteousness being accounted to us. R. C. has been willing to do whatever faithfulness requires so that the message remains clear, plain, straight, understood, and biblically faithful. That's why we asked him to speak on justification. He did so in a way that was helpful to pastors whose preaching may have wandered away to a focus other than the cross of Christ. We think you'll be blessed by reading his words.

And then there is that current evangelical rock star, John Piper! What a gift John is to the church. While too many of us are saying a lot of things quickly and running on to the next, John stops and stands and stays and stares at God's Word. Sometimes he stares at something that seems so obvious, but he keeps staring until it begins to expand and fill the horizon of his sight. It becomes rich and detailed and luscious and intricate and full and demanding and hope-giving and life-affirming and sin-denying and sacrifice-requiring—and adjective-adding. John prays and thinks until a part of God's Word which seemed simple and obvious becomes fresh and powerful.

The fruits of his labors were evidenced at the conference as he exhorted us not simply to inform people what God says in his Word but to exult in it. Preaching the cross without exulting in the cross is to deny the cross. That and much more await your attention in his chapter.

A Conference of Hope

Finally, we prayed to God for ourselves, our ministries, and for you who would enjoy the fruit of this labor. We enjoyed the opportunity to obey God's call by encouraging other ministers as we, too, were edified and encouraged. And now we have hopes and prayers for the readers of this volume. We desire you to preach the cross. Build your church by preaching the cross. Be encouraged and a source of encouragement by preaching the cross. Build friendships with ministers who preach the cross and with Christians who love God and are giving their whole lives to him. We pray that our cooperation will remind you of the largeness of God's plan, a plan that extends beyond our particular congregations or denominations. We hope that the Together for the Gospel Affirmation and Denials 2006 (appearing in this volume as Appendix) will be instructive and useful.

Learn from our Sovereign Grace guys to have confidence with humility. Learn from our Presbyterian friends to read books and conduct charitable, careful conversations. Learn from our nondenominational friends to center our unity in Christ and his gospel even more than in our traditions. And learn from us Baptists about . . . something. Since I am a Baptist, it wouldn't be seemly for me to finish *that* sentence!

Above all, as you read this book learn again to preach the cross. That is what a minister of the Word of God is called to do, from the New Testament and the Old, and in a way that is understandable and penetrating, faithful to the truth of justification by faith alone, visibly and verbally exulting in God's grace, reflected in our lives, and shown over the years and decades of ministry that God may give you. Preach the cross. That's why we came together. That's why we wrote this book. We pray that is what you're encouraged to do by reading it.

—Mark Dever, on behalf of Ligon Duncan,
C. J. Mahaney, and Albert Mohler

CHAPTER 1

A REAL MINISTER: 1 CORINTHIANS 4

Mark E. Dever

Churches today must be recovered. They must once again put the Word of God at the center; and that happens most fundamentally through preaching.

The great Puritan pastor Richard Baxter said that "All churches either rise or fall as the ministry doth rise or fall, not in riches and worldly grandeur, but in knowledge, zeal and ability for their work."[1] As I thought and prayed about the role of the pastor and the work of the ministry, my attention naturally turned to the situation at Corinth, where fake ministers were threatening to spoil the fruit of Paul's ministry. This crisis called forth from Paul some of his most pointed words and sustained meditations on the role of the pastor. In this chapter we will consider particularly chapter 4 of 1 Corinthians as we ponder what it means to be a real minister.

In 1 Corinthians 4 there is a striking contrast between the real ministers of Christ and the fake ones, the impostors. As we turn

---

[1] Marcus Loane, *Makers of Puritan History* (Grand Rapids, MI: Baker, 1961), 188.

to the passage, we find a pastor defining his role by means of three marks of a real minister.

The First Mark of a Real Minister Is a Cross-centered Message: 1 Corinthians 4:1–7

Paul writes, "So then, men ought to regard us as servants of Christ and as those entrusted with the secret things of God." (1 Cor. 4:1).[2] "The secret things of God"—that's what a real minister is all about. And that's why, Paul says, these Corinthians shouldn't divide over competing loyalties toward different ministers or preachers of the true gospel. If it is the gospel that has truly brought the congregation in Corinth together, then they will know unity rather than division among the various ministers of that same gospel.

Of course, they (the Corinthians) are not the ones appointed to be the final judges of God's ministers. Undergirding this situation at Corinth is an important principle: It is God's prerogative, and his alone, to judge ministers, because everything is done according to his purposes. Ministers of the gospel especially are stewards of God's mysteries, his secret things—the gospel. A steward is someone who is not an owner but one who is entrusted with someone else's property. So ministers must remember that the churches they lead are not theirs, regardless of how long they have been there. The entire church is the Lord's church, and God has entrusted his servants with the message of the crucified Messiah.

Paul wanted the Corinthians to understand that these servants, the preachers, would all be judged by whether they were faithful to their master—and their master wasn't the Corinthian congregation, and it certainly wasn't the worldly standards that seemed to control them. Look again at verse 1: "So then, men ought to regard us as servants of Christ and as those entrusted with the secret things

---

[2] Unless otherwise noted, Scripture references in this chapter are taken from the *New International Version of the Bible* (NIV).

of God." Even the apostles were ministers, not masters! They were fundamentally servants, not of the Corinthians but of Christ. As Matthew Henry put it, "They had no authority to propagate their own fancies, but to spread Christian faith."[3] They were sent out to preach the gospel and so see churches created.

Why does the postal service exist? What do we pay mailmen to do? Do we pay them to write letters to us and put them in our mailboxes? No. We pay them to deliver faithfully the message of someone else. The mailman has been entrusted with other people's messages to us. The same is true with ministers and their ministries. We are not to invent the message but to faithfully deliver God's message to his people. That is our calling, which means that we are called as ministers only insofar as we present God's message to his people. It is God who owns the church, and it is by his Word that he creates his people.

While attending a reception in Washington, I had a conversation with a Roman Catholic friend about a recently published book that we had both read. I asked him what he thought. "Oh, it was very good," he said, "except that it was marred by the author's repeating of that old Protestant error that the Bible created the church, when we all know," my friend said with assurance, "that the church created the Bible."

I was in a quandary. How should I respond? What should I say? But I decided that if he could be so openly dismissive, then I could be as contradictory as I wished. "That's ridiculous," I said, trying to sound as pleasant as I could. "God's people have never created God's Word! From the very beginning, God's Word has created his people. We see this in Genesis 1, where God literally created all that is by his Word, including his people. We see it in Genesis 12, where God calls Abraham out of Ur by the Word of

---

[3] *Matthew Henry's Commentary on the Whole Bible, Vol. 6: Acts to Revelation* (rpt. McLean, VA: MacDonald, n.d.), 522.

his promise. We find it in Ezekiel 37, where God gives Ezekiel a vision to share with the Israelite exiles in Babylon about a great resurrection that will come about by God's Word. In John 1 we see the supreme coming of God's Word in Jesus Christ, his Word made flesh. And in Romans 10 where we read that faith and spiritual life come by the Word, it is again clear that God has always created his people by his Word." It's never been the other way around!

I can't exactly remember what happened through the remainder of our conversation, but this portion of it certainly helped to gel some of my own understanding of the absolute centrality of the Word. The understanding I speak of is not simply an abstract one of how God has worked but one that influences our priorities in ministry in practical ways.

Consider the promotional mail pastors receive. The advertisements assure us success in ministry if we buy a particular product. No matter whether it's audio equipment, music, curriculum, a conference, or parking consulting, investing our money will make all the difference between our ministry's succeeding or failing. Many people have an economic interest in making us feel guilty, inadequate, and unequipped. The way to avoid such a snare is by convincing ourselves of the priority and the sufficiency of the ministry of the Word and to stake our whole service on that.

Do you see how important this is for the glory of God and the good of his people? Why, in so many of our churches, is it *unusual* to see someone giving their all to follow Christ, and growing in him? Is it because we allowed people who are in open unrepentant sin to continue on in our congregation, and so have diluted the witness, the fellowship? Why have we so neglected church discipline? Is it because we've not followed biblical instructions on leadership in the congregation (which we need in order to successfully practice church discipline), and we've also neglected the Bible's clear teaching on church discipline itself? Why have we neglected discipline? Is it because we don't teach about what church *mem-*

bership entails? And why would that be? Because we haven't made it clear what it really means to be a Christian in the first place? And why would that be? Because we've misunderstood the gospel? How could that be? Because we have misunderstood the Bible? And why would that be the case? Because we've had pastors who—with the best of motives—have given themselves to everything in the world before giving themselves to the study and preaching of God's Word! We've spent more time reading our email than our Bible. We have defended the Bible's authority more than experienced its power in our own lives.

Ministers are servants and stewards of God's Word—that's the message we are to deliver. We are stewards of the church in caring for a congregation; we don't own the church. *Steward* is a great word for a minister, isn't it? We are God's employees; he is our boss, and we work ultimately for him. The main task he has given us is making known the secret things of God—the gospel of the crucified Messiah!

Above everything else, a steward is called to be faithful. Paul continues, "It is required that those who have been given a trust must prove faithful" (1 Cor. 4:2). Paul's statement was an implicit condemnation of any unfaithful teacher among the Corinthians. The apostle Peter stated that all Christians are stewards, but ministers especially must be trustworthy (1 Pet. 4:10). We teachers of God's Word will be held accountable to a stricter judgment (James 3:1). We are like bankers, entrusted with a great deposit, and so we ministers of the Word must be faithful in our work because of the great value of what has been committed to us. Reliability, not originality, must be our concern as we recount the gospel of Christ crucified.

If the Corinthians thought less of Paul because of his commitment to this message, if other people dismissed him, if Paul himself even began to stray from it—none of these had commissioned him, and so none of these had the authority to change the message that had been entrusted to him. God alone was to determine what Paul did as a minister of his gospel.

Paul says here that "I care very little if I am judged by you or by any human court; indeed, I do not even judge myself. My conscience is clear, but that does not make me innocent. It is the Lord who judges me" (1 Cor. 4:3–4). Paul is unaware of anything against himself, but he knows that he is not acquitted by his self-assessment. It is the Lord who judges him. Of course, Paul isn't saying that self-examination is wrong; in fact, he calls for it later in this letter (9:24–27; cf. 2 Cor. 13:5), but our self-assessment—a clear conscience—simply isn't the ultimate issue. The nature of our fallenness is such that we can have a clear conscience and still be wrong, which is why our conscience must be educated by the Word of God. Self-esteem can't be the final arbiter of judgment because we esteem ourselves too highly! We are called to make provisional judgments (so Matt. 7:6)—as Paul is about to do forcefully in 1 Corinthians 5!—but no mere human is our ultimate judge because, as Paul says in 4:4, we will be judged by the Lord (cf. 2:10–16).

Do you see the freedom you have in knowing the identity of your ultimate judge—that there is only one and that he can be well-disposed toward you? The marvelous truth is that the One who knows us best is the One who loves us most. As Don Carson succinctly put it, "What matters most in God's universe is what God thinks of us."[4]

Assure yourself of God's verdict through Christ, and you can have a more accurate regard for the judgments of others (see v. 3). If you fear the Lord, you can deal with your fear of man. But remember that you cannot please God if you live to please men. I often think of a letter written by the Scottish pastor John Brown, which contained words of fatherly advice to a young man he had

---

[4]D. A. Carson, *From Triumphalism to Maturity* (Grand Rapids, MI: Baker, 1984), 80.

trained for the pastorate and who had recently been ordained as the minister of a small congregation. Brown wrote:

> I know the vanity of your heart, and that you will feel mortified that your congregation is very small, in comparison with those of your brethren around you; but assure yourself on the word of an old man, that when you come to give an account of them to the Lord Christ, at his judgment-seat, you will think you have had enough.[5]

Can you hear the echoes of the minister-as-steward in those words? Remember this also: "Obey your leaders and submit to their authority. They keep watch over you as men who must give an account" (Heb. 13:17).

A true minister of Christ, according to Paul, is one who lives to please Christ, the one and only coming judge. That's the time for ultimate judgment, not now and not by these Corinthians. "Therefore judge nothing before the appointed time; wait till the Lord comes. He will bring to light what is hidden in darkness and will expose the motives of men's hearts. At that time each will receive his praise from God" (1 Cor. 4:5; cf. 3:13). Perhaps the Corinthians were tempted to wrongly esteem teachers impressive by worldly standards or striking in external appearance and manner.

In Washington eloquent spokesmen are hired to speak on behalf of particular men and women whether or not they agree with the opinions they represent. But the confidence of the spokesmen lies in the greatness of their skills rather than in the truth of their message. In ancient Corinth eloquent orators were also prized, and they were celebrated, honored, and well paid. The regard for such speakers had crept into the church—men were hon-

---

[5] James Hay and Henry Belfrage, *Memoirs of the Rev. Alexander Waugh* (Edinburgh: William Oliphant and Son, 1839), 64–65.

ored not for giving the message of the cross but for how well they presented themselves, regardless of their actual message.

But such skills must not be the basis of evaluation for a Christian minister! For that reason, it is incredibly inappropriate, according to Paul, to allow a worldly, comparative pride of one Christian teacher over another. If each is a true Christian teacher, then each has been commissioned by the same master with the same message for the same purpose—glorifying God by proclaiming his reign. Allowing partisanship, as the Corinthians were, was to lose sight of the value of this one message. They were distracted by various messengers and their particular gifts. When such distraction occurs, we don't have far to go until we are following a particular messenger rather than the Word of God.

Brother, do you think you will be the last pastor called by your church? Are you leading the congregation toward loyalty to you or to God's Word and Christ's gospel? We pastors must be very careful about the loyalties we cultivate in the temporary stewardships we hold.

Paul continues, "Now, brothers, I have applied these things to myself and Apollos for your benefit, so that you may learn from us the meaning of the saying, 'Do not go beyond what is written.' Then you will not take pride in one man over against another" (1 Cor. 4:6). Scholars are uncertain about the origin of this quotation beyond the fact that it seemed to be well known. Most likely it was a reference to the expression, "it is written," used in the New Testament to quote the Old Testament. So it seems that Paul is exhorting the Corinthians not to go beyond the text of Scripture, and in so doing, he encourages the Corinthians to be committed to the message and to cherish faithfulness in their preachers.

We should be careful to remember that, as ministers, we are to be esteemed as instruments pointing to Christ. We must be faithful to deliver this particular message. Paul and Apollos were not in competition, as Paul carefully explained to the Corinthians in the opening chapters of this letter, because the gifts of God's ministers come directly from God: "For who makes you different from anyone else? What do you have that you did not receive? And if you did receive it, why do you boast as though you did not?" (1 Cor. 4:7).

These three questions have been some of the most important questions in the Bible down through the history of Christianity. From Augustine to Martin Luther, God has used this verse to affect people powerfully, humble them, and exalt himself. Let this question echo in your own soul for a little while: "What do you have that you did not receive?"

The last Sunday night of his life, John Knox reported that he was tempted by Satan to trust in himself and to rejoice or boast in himself, but, Knox said to his servant, "I repulsed him with this sentence: 'What do you have that you did not receive?'"[6] Earlier in the letter Paul had written about boasting: "Let him who boasts boast in the Lord" (1:31).

What do we have to boast about more than the cross of Christ, by which God has satisfied his love and his justice, his mercy and his holiness, and displayed it to all the world as he saves all who trust in him? A real minister has the cross at the center of his message, and his delivery of this message is the center of his role as a minister.

The Second Mark of a Real Minister Is a Cross-centered Life

C. J. Mahaney addresses well the cross-centered life in a later chapter where he considers Paul's words on the subject to Timothy. But the cross is an integral part of Paul's instructions to the Corinthians too, and it involves discerning which teachers they should trust. Paul refers to the apostles as "like men condemned

---

[6] Thomas M'Crie, *The Life of John Knox* (Philadelphia: Presbyterian Board of Publication, 1989), 338.

to die" (1 Cor. 4:9), and that was Paul's experience. This true apostle led a Christ-like life in stark contrast to the Corinthians, who saw prosperity as the mark of a true teacher. In this section of his letter, Paul uses some very sharp, ironic questions to deflate their pride and to reorient them to the cross and what Christ himself had taught about the nature of discipleship.

The use of heavy irony and a number of sarcastic statements are not Paul's normal manner of teaching. But such irony and occasional sarcasm are not always outside the bounds of appropriate communication. In fact, irony could be particularly useful in helping the Corinthians to see how the false apostles had confused them and how topsy-turvy their view of the Christian life had become. Paul launches in: "Already you have all you want! Already you have become rich! You have become kings—and that without us! How I wish that you really had become kings so that we might be kings with you!" (1 Cor. 4:8). Paul is mocking the Corinthians' prosperity. Some of it may have been real prosperity, some imagined. Either way, it's clear that many in the Corinthian church were feeling confident and fulfilled in a worldly manner.

Yet regardless of how they felt, Paul calls them back to reality and the truth that they weren't reigning. Perhaps the Corinthians had accepted a false notion of the Second Coming, which confused final glorification with spiritual life on this earth. But Paul points out that if this life is the final kingdom promised by God, then Christ's apostles certainly have no place in it if they are condemned to die in public shame: "For it seems to me that God has put us apostles on display at the end of the procession, like men condemned to die in the arena. We have been made a spectacle to the whole universe, to angels as well as to men" (4:9).

Paul's outlook on life and ministry was apparently a bit more humble than that of the Corinthians, which is revealed in his use of images from public processions and spectacles. In ancient military processions, the ones last in line were the prisoners, and of this number the last in line was the lowest in rank and the most despised. The reason for this is clear; such parades were filthy—the animals left their mark, and those farthest back in the procession had more of the accumulated remains to wade through. That, says Paul, has been his experience of life on earth, which is very different from the "reigning" the believers at Corinth claimed to be doing. Ultimately, such processions led to Corinth's theater, which seated eighteen thousand, and the most wretched of men—those last in line—were left for the last show, the last "spectacle" of the day. Paul uses this imagery in his letter to express how he feels.

How different is this life from what the Corinthians had been taught by imposter apostles! "We are fools for Christ, but you are so wise in Christ! We are weak, but you are strong! You are honored, we are dishonored!" (v. 10). Paul sarcastically contrasted himself with the Corinthians' claims. Paul understood that he was foolish (in the world's eyes), weak, and dishonored. But at least some of the Corinthians were fancying themselves to be wise, strong, and honored. They had cobbled together some illusions or replaced the cross as the center of the Christian life with something much more palatable. Matthew Henry thinks they were self-deceived: "Those do not commonly know themselves best who think best of themselves."[7]

I wonder what you think of yourself. The Christian message of a crucified Christ calls us to a different goal than we would otherwise pursue in this life. We're no longer concerned with what the world calls *wise*, those who made the decision to crucify Christ. We no longer live for what the world, which opposes God, calls *strength*. We're not captivated by applause and honor from those who have rejected Jesus, "the wisdom from God" (1 Cor. 1:30). My pastor friend, if you've been living for worldly wisdom and worldly honor,

---

[7] *Matthew Henry's Commentary on the Whole Bible, Vol. 6: Acts to Revelation*, 524.

aren't you beginning to notice how unsatisfying it is? There is a better way, and, strange as it may sound, Paul is setting it out here.

The true Christ was rejected and put to death on the cross. And it is only that Christ who actually saves us:

> Surely he took up our infirmities and carried our sorrows, yet we considered him stricken by God, smitten by him, and afflicted. But he was pierced for our transgressions, he was crushed for our iniquities; the punishment that brought us peace was upon him, and by his wounds we are healed. We all, like sheep, have gone astray, each of us has turned to his own way; and the LORD has laid on him the iniquity of us all. (Isa. 53:4–6)

If the One whom we follow was stricken, smitten, and afflicted, if he was pierced, crushed, punished, and wounded, then we can't be too surprised that some of that may happen to us in this world. The Christian ministry is not all attending conferences—let alone speaking at them! So we might expect such rejection to happen especially to Christ's ministers, not because we die to bear sin, but because in our lives, we live in a way this world rejects.

True ministers of Christ are happy to be despised, if, by their being despised, somehow the gospel is displayed. Our goal is to display the gospel of Jesus Christ. As Paul would later write to the Corinthians (quoting the Lord's response denying his request), "'My grace is sufficient for you, for my power is made perfect in weakness.' Therefore I will boast all the more gladly about my weaknesses, so that Christ's power may rest on me. That is why, for Christ's sake, I delight in weaknesses, in insults, in hardships, in persecutions, in difficulties. For when I am weak, then I am strong" (2 Cor. 12:9–10).

We know the bargain summarized by Jim Elliot: "He is no fool who gives what he cannot keep to gain what he cannot lose." Remember what Paul wrote: "The foolishness of God is wiser than man's wisdom, and the weakness of God is stronger than man's strength." (1 Cor. 1:25). True ministers of Christ and his cross have experienced this and are confident of it.

In his life Paul shared in the rejection of Christ: "To this very hour we go hungry and thirsty, we are in rags, we are brutally treated, we are homeless" (1 Cor. 4:11). The verbs in verses 11–12 are in the present tense, which means that Paul knew hunger and thirst as a present experience, even during the writing of this epistle. He wasn't reaching out from a great cathedral or a cushy university lectureship. Paul comes across more like an evacuee here! But, of course, his hope wasn't meant to be anchored here in this world. He, like all real Christian ministers, had his hope stored elsewhere.

Paul continues, "We work hard with our own hands. When we are cursed, we bless; when we are persecuted, we endure it; when we are slandered, we answer kindly" (vv. 12–13). The apostles have become the scum of the earth, the refuse of the world. Paul works with his hands (see Acts 18:3), preaches the gospel, experiences rejection from this world, and keeps on going even when his clothes are threadbare and his body exhausted. Remember, Paul worked as a tentmaker in Corinth (Acts 18:3). The worldly-wise, well-to-do citizens of Corinth would have been embarrassed to ask their friends to come and hear someone who earned a living by manual labor, someone such as Paul. But that didn't stop Paul from continuing on. Clearly he did not live for the approval of this world like the false ministers were doing.

When society cursed Paul, or persecuted and slandered him, they weren't taking from him anything he expected to keep in this world. Paul believed he had no right to well-wishes from God-haters and no ultimate right to freedom or a good name among those who rejected Christ. Yet he continued to respond to such opposition in the way Christ had demonstrated to his followers: "When they hurled their insults at him, he did not retaliate; when he suffered, he made no threats. Instead, he entrusted himself to him who judges justly" (1 Pet. 2:23; see also Matt. 5:10–12; Luke 6:28; 23:34).

Paul did not attempt to cover over opposing views of God and the world; he simply followed the one who said, "Foxes have holes and birds of the air have nests, but the Son of Man has no place to lay his head" (Luke 9:58; cf. Phil. 3:10). Paul wrote to the Romans: "If we are children, then we are heirs—heirs of God and co-heirs with Christ, if indeed we share in his sufferings in order that we may also share in his glory" (Rom. 8:17). Brother pastors, the only way to follow Jesus is to die daily to self-devotion.

A few questions now for senior pastors in particular: When was the last time you inconvenienced yourself in order to serve others? Do you use others to serve yourself or yourself to serve others? You realize, don't you, that an over-concern for physical comfort can be an enemy of your soul? What have you found effective in undermining your concern for personal comfort— biographies, role models, accountability, or discipline? Have these tools produced visible fruit in your life and in the lives of others?

Prosperity isn't always wrong, but prosperity is always dangerous. It can be disorienting to the Christian, perhaps especially to the minister. We must live lives that show there are things that are worth even more than this world's prosperity. How can you do that in your circumstances this week?

Pray for me, that I would have a life that evidences the supremacy of Christ and his cross in my affections. Consider the biblical qualifications for eldership; do you aspire to reflect these qualifications? We want to live a life different from this world, a life that tells the truth, a life that gives hope in a dying world. Real ministers live cross-centered lives.

The Third Mark of a Real Minister Is Having Cross-centered Followers

In the middle of the next section of Paul's letter (1 Cor. 4:14–21), Paul writes, "Therefore I urge you to imitate me" (v. 16). This is

Paul's way of urging the Corinthians (his spiritual children) to humble themselves as the apostles (and Christ!) have done and to stop following the foolish ways of their worldly teachers. Paul warns them about the false way at least some of them seem to be taking and urges them to follow his example instead.

Paul exhibited no pride in putting himself forward as a model. In fact, he demonstrated humility by inviting personal scrutiny into a life—his—that Paul knew was far from perfect. Paul was a sinner, of course, but in-so-far as he followed Christ, he presented his life as a light for others to follow. Surely a Christian minister should not only teach the gospel correctly and live a Christ-like life, but he should also lead others to do the same. Models are a basic tool from which we grow and learn—children in families, kids on a team, apprentices in trade, and new Christians in church. Example is part of pastoral ministry.

Yet for all the severity of his language, you can see that Paul really loves these Corinthians. He had lived with them for a year and a half. "I am not writing this to shame you, but to warn you, as my dear children," he wrote (v. 14). Brother elder, do you feel like that about the members of your congregation? Paul's phrasing makes clear that he was aware of coming across harshly. But he loves them with fatherly love, as he goes on to explain: "Even though you have ten thousand guardians in Christ, you do not have many fathers, for in Christ Jesus I became your father through the gospel" (v. 15).

Paul reminds them that he is their father in the gospel in a unique way. He was the church planter at Corinth, the founding father of that local congregation (see Acts 18). We have special regard, don't we, for those whom God used to lead us to Christ? Paul was using their regard—he was using anything he could—to dissuade these young believers from following imitation teachers and their counterfeit gospel, which is also why he urges them outright to imitate him[8] He holds out his arms through this letter and appeals to them with the voice of a father for their trust to imitate him in living a cross-centered life.

Children naturally imitate their parents, but calling upon adults to a lifestyle of imitation certainly puts on pressure—hopefully of the right kind! Just like Paul, Christian preachers are models. There's no way around it; modeling is part of our calling. Paul had been the example the Corinthians followed until other teachers came along with an initially attractive, alternative example.

Some time ago I had the privilege of dining with a fellow board member at the Alliance of Confessing Evangelicals, Dr. C. Everett Koop. Dr. Koop was President Reagan's surgeon general from 1981–1989. At one point, dinner conversation turned to good nutrition, and someone made a comment about Dr. Koop's dinner order. He responded that in his role as surgeon general he was paid to be a teacher, not an example! Of course, he was joking, but there is no doubt that pastors should be examples. We serve Christ as ministers of his Word, which should be accompanied by a life that acts as a sounding board to ratify and verify our teaching and strongly push it out even farther.

Of course, we will never be faithful ministers if we only preach what we live perfectly; nevertheless, we should generally be examples to the flock God has committed to our care. We must be sure that not only are we prayed for, loved, obeyed, and supported, but also that our examples are followed. Writing as a preacher, and at least a little aware of my own sins, this is a harrowing responsibility. But it is an unavoidable part of the job. If I'm going to preach the Bible, I have to preach more than I can live, though I should always be trying to live, by God's grace, so as to be an example of Christ's power in my life and an encouragement to others.

---

[8] Paul says similar things elsewhere. See, for example, 1 Cor. 11:1; Gal. 4:12; Phil. 3:17; 1 Thess. 1:6; 2 Thess. 3:7, 9; cf. Heb. 13:7.

Reinforcing what he has just written, Paul adds, "For this reason I am sending to you Timothy, my son whom I love, who is faithful in the Lord. He will remind you of my way of life in Christ Jesus, which agrees with what I teach everywhere in every church" (v. 17). Timothy would teach them how to live faithfully.

In light of his difficult circumstances, I'm sure it was hard for Paul to send away a close friend and co-laborer such as Timothy, so the fact that he did shows something of the depth of his love for them. Paul had an intense desire for the Corinthians to be taught the truth about Christ and see Christ-like teachers live out the faith before them, and for that reason he wouldn't rest well until he knew that they better and more fully embodied the Christianity they professed.

That's why he says what he does here at the end of chapter 1 about his upcoming visit, where he challenges the Corinthians to be ready to see him. Some of these believers had become arrogant, as Paul sharply points out (v. 18), so he is, in effect, ordering them to be humble! Did you realize that humility is your duty if you're a follower of Christ, especially if you've been entrusted with any authority in the congregation? Humility encourages every other virtue, it undermines our sin, and it opens us up to hearing how we can continue to grow in Christ.

Consider the importance of authority, and how it is subjected to unending suspicion and critique these days. However, such critique is not unique to our postmodern, post-Enlightenment culture. Suspecting authority is the very heart of the fall. Satan essentially convinced our first parents that God could not tell us "no" and love us at the same time. The first sin was born when Eve accepted the lie that a denial of desire cannot flow from good, loving, and correct care.

A natural suspicion of authority is one reason that those of us who carry it in various spheres should exercise it carefully. Abuse of authority seems to validate the basic human decision to deny

God's fatherly role in our lives. It also gives the enemy another tool,
another charge, another example. Authority is a wonderful, life-
giving gift (see 2 Sam. 23:3–4), which can and must be used. But
authority should only be used with sincere humility.

How could we ever imagine following Christ without continual growth in humility? Who could be more humble than Christ?
How can we think to follow him in his self-giving love unless our
self-concerns shrink while our concerns about God and others
grow?

Consider how Paul finishes this section of his letter:

> But I will come to you very soon, if the Lord is willing, and then
> I will find out not only how these arrogant people are talking, but
> what power they have. For the kingdom of God is not a matter
> of talk but of power. What do you prefer? Shall I come to you
> with a whip, or in love and with a gentle spirit? (1 Cor. 4:19–21)

Paul is clear that he will come and investigate the claims of the arrogant among them,[9] and he says that when he comes, he will investigate not their words, but their power, because the kingdom of
God is not about words but about power. God's rulership or reign
isn't just an idea—it happens in people's lives. It is happening in the
lives of many reading this chapter and in our congregations.

Paul is challenging the Corinthians to consider the results of
false teachers. Is their teaching producing anything more than hot
air or are people actually being saved through their message? In this
last verse Paul warns that if they do not respond to his gentle love,
he will come with a whip, by which, of course, he means not a lit-
eral whip, but a severe reproof. Both gentleness and severity are a
part of Christian love, and especially of the love of the minister
for his congregation.

---

[9] It's interesting that Paul says he will do this "if the Lord is willing." It's as if he had read James's
letter (James 4:15). Even apostles are humbled when they consider the future!

Brothers, as Paul said elsewhere, our congregations are the proof of our ministry. We need congregations comprised of people whose lives reflect the truth of the gospel that we preach. One friend of mine particularly likes icons—images of the prophets, apostles, even Jesus Christ. He explains his devotion to icons by the same reasoning that Eastern Orthodox theologians have used for more than a thousand years—if we don't have images of Christ, they reason, that must be rooted in a flesh-denying Gnosticism, and we, in effect, are denying the incarnation.

I, for one, am not persuaded. Jesus didn't train his disciples in sketching or painting. The first image we have of Christ was written by a pagan mocking a Christian "worshiping his god"—and the little crude drawing has a simple figure with a donkey's head hanging on a cross. If we had a photograph of Jesus and the twelve disciples, I don't think we could tell which one was Jesus merely by his appearance. No glow; no halos. On the other hand, if that picture were to become a moving picture, then I think we could tell the identity of Christ very quickly by noticing which one gave himself in love to those around him. The sacrifice of love—that was the purpose of the incarnation, and that is the purpose of the church. God has left a witness for himself in you and in our congregations. Our physical natures are an aspect of our social natures, enabling our ability to interact with others in love and service.

Jesus said in John 13, "A new command I give you: Love one another. As I have loved you, so you must love one another. By this all men will know that you are my disciples, if you love one another" (vv. 34–35). God has forbidden statues to be made of him; Jesus had no icons of himself drawn and painted, but by his Spirit he fashions a representation of himself—and that is the church. In its holiness we see something of God's holiness; in its unity we see something of God's unity; in its love, we see something of God's love.

Looking back over 1 Corinthians 4, I'm struck by the great

combination of humility and confidence Paul displayed in his words and life, which make him a model for all of us. We should desire boldness for helping others grow in Christ. We ought to risk ourselves in order to be of service to others.

That's what Paul was challenging the Corinthians to look for, surrounded as they were by imposters: a cross-centered message, a cross-centered life, and cross-centered followers.

Conclusion

The most important issue for recovering churches is placing the Word at the center, and that happens most fundamentally through preaching. Now it's one thing to hear and cheer such talk at a conference, or to root for it in the privacy of our office while reading a book; it is another to live it out in our ministries. The congregations to which God has called us are of much greater importance than any conference or book. Ministers who write books and speak at conferences know that doing so falls outside of our normal work in ministry and calling, and that such ministries are not our most important charge. But serving in these venues enables us to exercise congregational stewardship.

By his last question, Paul was telling the Corinthians that how they prepared for his coming would determine the tone of the visit. The choice that stands before us is very much like the choice Paul gave to them. Your life will soon be intersected by God, whether through the Lord's return or your death. And how will that coming be for you? Will you find yourself prepared by the truth about the cross, or will you find yourself caught out, unprepared, living—even in your pastorate—as if this passing world were going to last forever?

My brother pastor, beware the siren call of those teachers who beckon you to put your heart—your all—into the priorities of this world. They are impostors; they are lying to you. The wolves don't come with business cards that say *wolf*. Jesus taught that the wolves would dress up to look like sheep. They learn sheep language and use sheep expressions. They even publish books with sheep publishers, all so that you will think they're sheep. But be wise. Look at their message—what are they saying?

The great news is about another home, an immortal one, available to you. Its power streams back into this life, to which Paul's life and teaching gave witness. The cross is the center, but it's not the end. Jesus endured the cross for the joy set before him. And we are called to be his followers. On through the cross of this world's rejection is the eternal acceptance of God. You can have no better goal than to be in a loving relationship forever with this great and glorious God and to lead others into the same. Our churches are to be living, loving, moving pictures of this great gospel. Preaching this gospel, leading a church to be such a display, is our real ministry.

CHAPTER 2

PREACHING CHRIST FROM THE OLD TESTAMENT

J. Ligon Duncan III

"You, however, continue in the things you have learned and become convinced of, knowing from whom you have learned them, and that from childhood you have known the sacred writings which are able to give you the wisdom that leads to salvation through faith which is in Christ Jesus. All Scripture is inspired by God and profitable for teaching, for reproof, for correction, for training in righteousness; so that the man of God may be adequate, equipped for every good work" (2 Tim. 3:14–16).[1]

One of the encouraging signs found among many young Christians today is a renewed appetite for expository preaching. By expository preaching I don't mean one particular style or method of preaching, but a self-conscious, principled commitment to preaching in such a way that the Scripture itself is supplying the main theme, principle headings, and central application in our proclamation.

Young people are looking for churches where the Bible is

---

[1] Unless otherwise noted, Scripture references in this chapter are taken from *The New American Standard Bible* (NASB).

preached. They are tired of (and not a little cynical about) dumbed-down preaching or preaching that is too clever by half. Young people can detect preaching that uses a text of Scripture as an excuse for talking about something else or as a mere launching point but is then ignored during the remainder of the message or deployed in such a way as to make medieval allegorists look like the most rigorous of exegetes! The kind of preaching that has been advocated by those who viewed the seeker movement as the cutting edge of kingdom advancement—Scripture-anemic, superficially practical, therapeutic, man-centered, God-at-your-service, consumer-driven fireside chats—is death on the ears of legions of younger Bible-believing Christians today. They want the real stuff—no-holds-barred, high-octane, meaty exposition of God's inspired word—applied until it hurts.

For that reason it is also encouraging to see hosts of young evangelical pastors newly committed to the practice of expository preaching. Many of them even prefer preaching through Bible books, and for this I praise God. But I have also noted in the midst of this general revival of expository preaching a neglect of the Old Testament. While you can hear many fine sermons in many fine evangelical churches on the Epistles and Gospels, a series on Genesis, Exodus, the Psalms, or the Minor Prophets is much rarer.

That is why we are taking up the topic of preaching Christ from the Old Testament. We want to learn how God, in the New Testament, exhorts us, as ministers of the new covenant, to preach from the Old Testament, because he has given all of Scripture for his people's edification. In keeping with this I want to offer eight simple exhortations to you.

1) Preach the Old Testament

It is hard to imagine that Christian pastors of a different era would even have thought to include this in a discussion on preaching—much less make it their first point. But we live in a different time with different practices and different inherited habits, and one of those habits, in so many churches, is to downplay or even ignore the Old Testament in the ministry of preaching. So we must begin by encouraging one another to preach the Old Testament, and I might add as an addition to that phrase, to preach the Old Testament as a Christian book.

The apostle Paul urged Timothy to do just that in this passage. Paul refers to "the sacred writings" that Timothy had known since the very days of his youth (v. 15). Now those sacred writings that Timothy had known from the days of his youth were not the Gospels or the Epistles or the book of Revelation. They were the Old Testament Scriptures, from Genesis to Malachi, which he had known from the days of his youth.

So when Paul goes on to say that "all Scripture is inspired by God and profitable for teaching, for reproof, for correction, for training in righteousness" (v. 16), he has in his sights the Old Testament. Now we are exactly right to extend to the whole of Scripture, both Old Testament and New, the qualities that Paul describes here in this passage. Indeed, Paul himself, as he is speaking about the care of elders, designates both old and new covenant Scripture as authoritative when he says: "The elders who rule well are to be considered worthy of double honor, especially those who work hard at preaching and teaching. For the Scripture says, 'You shall not muzzle the ox while he is threshing,' and 'The laborer is worthy of his wages'" (1 Tim. 5:17–18).

Notice how in that one verse the apostle Paul manages to quote from Deuteronomy and from a dominical saying recorded by Luke and call them both "Scripture." So the apostle Paul's words about the inspiration of all Scripture certainly applies to the totality of the canon of Scripture—Old Testament and New Testament. The apostle Paul is saying to Timothy, "Timothy, you have known the sacred writings, the Old Testament from Genesis to Malachi, from your youth. Take that Scripture and teach it. Take that Scripture and exhort from it. Take that Scripture and preach to God's people the way of salvation by faith alone in Christ alone from the Old Testament Scripture." The apostle Paul is urging Timothy to preach the Scriptures of the Old Testament as a Christian book.

It is important for us to grasp that so much of the New Testament is a hermeneutical manual to help Christians understand the Old Testament and to help Christian preachers understand how to preach and apply the Old Testament. This was not lost on the early Christian fathers.

Let's imagine an approaching Easter Sunday sometime in the middle of the second century when one of the great church fathers, Melito of Sardis, is preparing to preach a message at a service where many converts will be baptized. He wants to preach a message that exalts the work of Christ on his cross on behalf of sinners. And so he naturally chooses—that's right—Exodus 12(!), as so many early Christian preachers did in the second century.

Why? Because they understood that Jesus was the Passover Lamb, that the Old Testament is a book about Christ, and that the Old Testament is Christian Scripture. We lost Melito's sermon for about 1,800 years, and then in the first half of the twentieth century, we discovered *Peri Pascha*, ("On the Passover," or "On the Passover Lamb," or "On Easter"). It is his exposition of the cross via Exodus 12. It is a new covenant exposition of an old covenant text.

Or you pick up Irenaeus's *Demonstration of the Apostolic Preaching*, another important second-century work, and he will walk you through the Old Testament and this glorious plan of God's redemption, which is unfolding from Adam all the way through Malachi and then into the New Testament. Irenaeus understood, with the rest of the church fathers, that new covenant believers need to be apprised of their old covenant legacy. Christians need to be preached from, taught, and instructed in the riches of the Old Testament.

One formidable contemporary theologian puts it this way:

> We must plant our feet firmly on the rock of the absolute author-
> ity of the Old Testament. It was precisely these Holy Scriptures
> that Paul described as inspired. Curiously, he does not say that
> the writers were inspired. He says that the books were inspired.
> They were breathed out by God. Nor is this true merely of some
> portions of the Old Testament. It was all inspired. Some parts
> may be less interesting, less majestic and even less useful than
> others, but every single part is inspired.
>
> What any Old Testament Scripture says, God says. This
> means at once that the entire Old Testament must be handled
> with reverence. It is all holy. It also means that the preacher
> has to interpret it harmonistically. He cannot set one part
> against another. He cannot contrast any part of it with the truth.
> As a word from God, it must hang together coherently and har-
> monize with all that we know from the other sources. For the
> same reason, the preacher knows that the whole Old Testament
> is profitable; its usefulness is coexistent with its inspiration. This
> applies even to those parts of it which have been superseded,
> such as the civil law of Israel, and the cultic arrangements asso-
> ciated with tabernacle and temple. The detailed instructions laid
> down in these connections are no longer binding on the Church,
> yet they still serve to illustrate, symbolize, and typify important
> truths."[2]

And so, the apostle Paul says to Timothy and to us, we are to
preach the Old Testament and to preach it as a Christian book.

To put it another way, my dear friend Dr. Knox Chamblin,
longtime New Testament professor at Reformed Theological
Seminary, says: "combat your tendency to choose a canon within
the canon by purposing to preach 'the whole purpose of God'—
Moses as well as Mark, Jonah as well as John, Psalms as well as
Paul, Proverbs as well as Peter, Leviticus as well as Luke,

---

[2] Donald Macleod, *Monthly Record of the Free Church of Scotland*, editorial (February 1984).

Habakkuk as well as Hebrews, Ruth as well as Revelation. Think how Paul's celebration of Pentecost, in Acts 2:16, will be enriched by joining the instructions of Leviticus 23 to the event of Acts 2."

2) Preach the Old Testament Expositionally

Notice again what the apostle Paul emphasizes in 2 Timothy 3:16: all Scripture is inspired, all Scripture is profitable. He has already laid down there the principle of *tota Scriptura*. We all believe in *sola Scriptura*, that the Scriptures of the Old and the New Testament, the very words of God, are the final rule of faith and practice for the believer. It is the only authoritative measure of all else in Christian life and belief. But it is not only the final authority—it is also that the whole of the Scripture is that final authority. The apostle Paul is urging Timothy to preach from all of the Old Testament.

The same point is made in Luke 24:27. It is one of the most beautiful encounters with the risen Savior recorded in the New Testament, as Jesus instructs the two discouraged disciples on the road to Emmaus. "Then beginning with Moses and with all the prophets, He explained to them the things concerning Himself in all the Scriptures."

So we see both Paul and Jesus urging the whole of the Old Testament Scriptures to be expounded and explained as Christian Scriptures. This is important for us to pursue also. In my own congregation we try to keep a balance between the preaching of the Old Testament and the New Testament as we schedule our sermons. We try to read or proclaim God's Word from a Gospel either on Sunday morning or Sunday evening or Wednesday night, either as a reading of Scripture or in the proclamation of the Word, but we also try to include an Old Testament book in one of these services as well.

So, for example, we move sequentially through Genesis to the first book of the Psalms, and Exodus to the second book of the Psalms, and Leviticus to the third book of the Psalms. At the time of this writing we are getting ready to launch into Numbers, and then we will come back to the fourth book of the Psalms. One day my congregation, long-suffering though they be, may, in fact, eventually arrive at Deuteronomy and then to the fifth book of the Psalms, along with our regular reading and preaching of the Gospels and letters from the New Testament.

You need to choose good preaching models. I would urge you first to listen to good preaching from the Old Testament, which is so widely available today. Then read solid Christian preachers expounding the Scriptures of the Old Testament. James Boice served us so well in this way.[3] But his successor, Philip Ryken, has been an outstanding model and example of preaching the Old Testament. If you have never looked at his massive commentaries on Exodus and Jeremiah, you've missed a feast for your soul.[4] Phil's work will give you an example of how to do extended expository preaching through those Old Testament books.

But all of us know that not all of our congregations can bear extended expository preaching through large Old Testament books. So if you pick up a copy of *The Message of the Old Testament* by our own Mark Dever, you will get an idea of how to preach overviews of Old Testament books.[5] The Lord has given us many tools, even in these last fifteen years, to help preachers preach expositionally through the Old Testament. Utilize those resources.

3) Preach Christ from the Old Testament

Do you remember the men who lamented in Luke 24? They had placed their hopes in Jesus, but their hopes had been dashed against the rocks. Jesus' response to them was "O foolish men and slow

[3] E.g., James Montgomery Boice, *Genesis: An Expositional Commentary,* 2 volumes (Grand Rapids, MI: Zondervan, 1985); *The Minor Prophets* (Grand Rapids, MI: Kregel, 1996).
[4] Philip Graham Ryken, *Exodus: Saved For God's Glory* (Wheaton, IL: Crossway, 2005); *Jeremiah & Lamentations: From Sorrow to Hope* (Wheaton, IL: Crossway, 2001).
[5] Mark Dever, *The Message of the Old Testament: Promises Made* (Wheaton, IL: Crossway, 2006).

of heart to believe in all that the prophets have spoken!" (v. 25). The Lord Jesus was utterly confident that had they listened to what the prophets had said, they would have heard about him. They would have heard about his person, his work, and the nature of the Messiah. So Jesus said, "'Was it not necessary for the Christ to suffer these things and to enter into His glory?' Then beginning with Moses and with all the prophets, He explained to them the things concerning Himself in all the Scriptures" (vv. 26–27).

We see there in Jesus' own exhortation and example that we are to preach Christ from the Old Testament, which is relatively easy to do when we have direct New Testament interpretation of Old Testament, christological passages. Consider Isaiah 6:

> I saw the Lord sitting on a throne, lofty and exalted, with the train of His robe filling the temple. Seraphim stood above Him, each having six wings: with two he covered his face, and with two he covered his feet, and with two he flew. And one called out to another and said, "Holy, Holy, Holy is the LORD of hosts, the whole earth is full of His glory." (Isa. 6:1–3)

When we preach from Isaiah 6 and expound the vision of Isaiah in the year of King Uzziah's death and his description of what he saw, the Bible gives us John's commentary on that passage. John tells us, in the context of explaining the rejection of Jesus Christ by his own people and contemporaries, that Isaiah was speaking of Jesus: "These things Isaiah said because he saw His glory, and he spoke of Him" (John 12:41).

We see the same principle when we go to passages like Psalm 118. "The stone which the builders rejected has become the chief corner stone. This is the LORD's doing; it is marvelous in our eyes. This is the day which the LORD has made. Let us rejoice and be glad in it" (vv. 22–24).

Now the early Christians used that as their call to worship on Easter Sunday: "This is the day the Lord has made. Let us rejoice and be glad in it." Why? Well, because they had read Acts 4:11, where the apostle Peter explains, speaking of "Jesus Christ, the Nazarene whom you crucified. . . . He is the stone which was rejected by you, the builders, but which became the chief corner stone." And so it is easy to preach Christ from the Old Testament when you have direct New Testament interpretation of those Old Testament christological passages.

But we ought to be able to preach Christ naturally and exegetically from all of the Old Testament. That does not mean that we force Christ in an odd way into places where he is not found in the Old Testament, but that we realize that there is always a way to Christ and to his cross from every passage in the Old Testament.

A number of years ago several men were undergoing examination for the ministry in my presbytery, and all of these men were required to give testimony of their Christian experience of salvation as well as their objective and subjective call to the ministry. The variety in their testimonies was remarkable, especially the manner in which they had come to faith in Christ. A couple of them had grown up in Christian homes. One had known, from the earliest days of his remembrances, that he was a sinner and needed a savior, and that Christ was that Savior; another had been reared in a Christian home but had rejected the teachings of his parents in the days of his youth, gone astray, and come back to the Lord by his marvelous grace. Yet another had come from a family that was not Christian; the young man did not read the Bible or attend church until he was in college, at which time he was brought to faith in Christ. Their stories of salvation were radically different.

At the end of that examination period, the clerk of presbytery, who happened to be the eldest minister there, stood up and said, "We've been reminded again today that though there is only one way to God, there are many ways to Christ." He meant that although salvation is through Jesus Christ and his cross alone, the Lord draws us to Christ in many different ways. Preaching Christ from the Old Testament is the same: there is only one way to God, which is through Jesus Christ, but there is a dazzling variety of ways to get to Christ in the Old Testament.

2 Samuel 7 is an extraordinarily important passage in which the Davidic covenant is formally inaugurated. The Lord God said to David:

> When your days are complete and you lie down with your fathers, I will raise up your descendant after you, who will come forth from you, and I will establish his kingdom. He shall build a house for My name, and I will establish the throne of his kingdom forever. I will be a father to him and he will be a son to Me; when he commits iniquity, I will correct him with the rod of men and the strokes of the sons of men, but My lovingkindness shall not depart from him, as I took it away from Saul, whom I removed from before you. Your house and your kingdom shall endure before Me forever; your throne shall be established forever. (2 Sam. 7:12–16)

It is an extraordinary passage. Saul had longed for his son Jonathan to sit on the throne, and God's word to Saul had been, "No, Saul, Jonathan will not sit on the throne." But to David, God said, "David, your son will sit on the throne. And, David, it is not just that your son will sit upon the throne, but I will not forsake him in the way that Saul was forsaken—he will sit on the throne forever."

It is a glorious passage. But, of course, it is a passage that caused great angst in the hearts of the Old Testament prophets in the days then the southern kingdom fell. Israel had fallen in the eighth century, the southern kingdom fell in the sixth century, and the prophets were left asking themselves, "How could it be that God's promise to David should fail? How could it be that there is not a descendant of David sitting on the throne? God promised that he would reign there forever, that his lovingkindness would never depart. Has the promise of God failed?"

Of course, David's dynasty was an extraordinarily long reign. While there were multiple capitals and multiple houses in the northern kingdom, there was one capital and one house in the southern kingdom for four hundred years—perhaps the longest single dynasty to reign in any country in the history of the world, all the more remarkable in the volatile Middle East. Yet the promise was not that David would reign for a long time, but that he would reign forever. The prophets, as they wrestled with this, were given the vision of the new covenant by the Holy Spirit.

When the people asked, "Can the promises fail? David's man is not on the throne," Jeremiah replied:

> "Behold, days are coming," declares the LORD, "when I will make a new covenant with the house of Israel and with the house of Judah, not like the covenant which I made with their fathers in the day I took them by the hand to bring them out of the land of Egypt, My covenant which they broke, although I was a husband to them," declares the LORD. "But this is the covenant which I will make with the house of Israel after those days," declares the LORD, "I will put My law within them and on their heart I will write it; and I will be their God, and they shall be My people. They will not teach again, each man his neighbor and each man his brother, saying, 'Know the LORD,' for they will all know Me, from the least of them to the greatest of them," declares the LORD, "for I will forgive their iniquity, and their sin I will remember no more." (Jer. 31:31–34)

This is the only time the term *new covenant* is used in all of the Old Testament prophetic literature, but the parallels to that passage are copious. Go to Isaiah, elsewhere in Jeremiah, or to Ezekiel, and you will see parallels to that passage. Observe how Ezekiel describes the same thing that Jeremiah is speaking of:

> "My servant David will be king over them, and they will all have one shepherd; and they will walk in My ordinances and

keep My statutes and observe them. They will live on the land
that I gave to Jacob My servant, in which your fathers lived;
and they will live on it, they, and their sons and their sons' sons,
forever; and David My servant will be their prince forever. I will
make a covenant of peace with them; it will be an everlasting
covenant with them. And I will place them and multiply them,
and will set My sanctuary in their midst forever. My dwelling
place also will be with them; and I will be their God, and they will
be My people. And the nations will know that I am the LORD
who sanctifies Israel, when My sanctuary is in their midst forever." (Ezek. 37:24–28)

The early Christians looked at that, and they said, "Jesus is David's
son." Jesus looked at his disciples and said, "I am David's greater
son. I am the fulfillment of that longing, because the kingship of
David pointed to an everlasting reign, the reign of the Messiah
King—and I am that Messiah."

The early Christians weren't just inventing some crazy spiritual-
ized exegesis; they had learned this from the lips of the apostle Peter:

And so, because he was a prophet and knew that God had sworn
to him with an oath to seat one of his descendants on His throne,
he looked ahead and spoke of the resurrection of the Christ,
that He was neither abandoned to Hades, nor did His flesh suffer decay. This Jesus God raised up again, to which we are all witnesses. Therefore having been exalted to the right hand of God,
and having received from the Father the promise of the Holy
Spirit, He has poured forth this which you both see and hear.
For it was not David who ascended into heaven, but he himself
says: "The LORD said to my Lord, 'Sit at my right hand, until I
make your enemies a footstool for your feet.'" Therefore let all
the house of Israel know for certain that God has made Him both
Lord and Christ—this Jesus whom you crucified. (Acts 2:30–36)

Do you see how Peter got from the promises of God to David
to Jesus? He didn't have to read Jesus back onto 2 Samuel 7 in

some stilted way. He simply unfolded the truth of God's redemptive plan in 2 Samuel 7, Jeremiah 31, and Ezekiel 37 and showed how it points us to Christ. Notice that Peter takes us not only to Christ, but to his cross and to his resurrection as well. Preach Christ from the Old Testament.

4) Preach the One Plan of Redemption from the Old Testament

Graeme Goldsworthy's book *Preaching the Whole Bible as Christian Scripture* (itself a distillation of some of Sidney Greidanus's insights), is helpful in teaching us to recognize redemptive history in our preaching.[6] Ed Clowney has also been a significant help to preachers who desire to reflect biblical theology and to preach Christ from the Old Testament.[7] But preaching the one plan of redemptive history from the Old Testament is simply a New Testament exhortation.

Notice how often the New Testament utilizes the formula, "This is that . . ." In other words, to explain *this* (the new covenant event or reality) is the fulfillment of *that* (the old covenant promise or prophecy). "This is that" preaching in the New Testament is tying together the whole of God's redemptive plan. We see this in Peter's preaching in Acts when he says, "This is what was spoken of through the prophet Joel . . ." (2:16; Joel 2). Peter ties together God's outworking of redemptive history from the old covenant to the new.

By the way, displaying the redemptive unity of the Old and New Testaments in preaching need not downplay in any way the discontinuity or the distinctions between the old covenant and new

---

[6] Graeme Goldsworthy, *Preaching the Whole Bible as Christian Scripture: The Application of Biblical Theology to Expository Preaching* (Grand Rapids, MI: Eerdmans, 2000). Greidanus's insights are found in *The Modern Preacher and the Ancient Text: Interpreting and Preaching Biblical Literature* (Grand Rapids, MI: Eerdmans, 1988); and in Sidney Greidanus, *Preaching Christ From the Old Testament: A Contemporary Hermeneutical Method* (Grand Rapids, MI: Eerdmans, 1999).

[7] E.g., Edmund P. Clowney, "Preaching Christ from All the Scriptures," in *Preachers & Preaching*, ed. Samuel T. Logan Jr. (Phillipsburg, NJ: P&R, 1986), 163–91; Clowney, *The Unfolding Mystery: Discovering Christ in the Old Testament* (Phillipsburg, NJ: P&R, 1991).

covenant realities; in fact, it glories in them. Recently, while reading through 2 Kings with my six-year-old son (and let me tell you, that is some gory stuff for a six-year-old; talk about wide-eyed attention!), I was struck with how thankful I am to live in the light of the gospel glory of the new covenant. However, at the same time, I was struck by the beautiful way in which this old covenant text was used by God's Spirit for gospel purposes in my son's life.

As we moved from Elijah to Elisha, we passed through the story, of course, of Gehazi's greed in 2 Kings 5. And my son and I had a long talk. He had a lot of questions. He asked, "Dad, Gehazi lied and God's judgment came on him, didn't it?"

"You are right, son," I replied.

"Dad, I sin too. God's judgment might come on me."

"Son, it's very, very important that you understand that."

"Dad, I don't want to sin, but sometimes I do. How will I escape from God's judgment?"

"Son, there is no more significant question that you can ask in this world than that. Let's talk about the gospel of the Lord Jesus Christ, and what it means to have faith in him."

There is opportunity for gospel conversation even in 2 Kings 5. But let me tell you, after working through Elijah and Elisha, the overwhelming thought I had was, "Lord, God, thank you that in your mercy I was brought into this world under the reign of Christ in his new covenant and that I did not have to live in those days."

We don't downplay the discontinuities, but we do see the strands, the one plan of redemptive history, from the Old to the New Testament. We see it in the beginning of the Bible. The Lord, even in his word of judgment against Eve, said, "I will put enmity between you and the woman, and between your seed and her seed; He shall bruise you on the head and you shall bruise Him on the heel" (Gen. 3:15). Do you understand that this God-established enmity, even in that word of judgment to Eve, is one of the great signs of how God takes the initiative with his sovereign grace in our salvation? There is a warfare between the woman and the enemy of her soul, and that divinely established warfare shows the initiative of God's sovereign grace in salvation, that he is working to keep the enemy of the woman's soul from destroying her, driving a wedge between that woman and the one who would devour her soul forever.

The whole of Genesis 3–11 is the unfolding of the story of those seeds. Then in Genesis 12:1–3 God's promise to Abram is spelled out:

> Now the LORD said to Abram, "Go forth from your country, and from your relatives and from your father's house, to the land which I will show you; and I will make you a great nation, and I will bless you, and make your name great; and so you shall be a blessing; and I will bless those who bless you, and the one who curses you I will curse. And in you all the families of the earth will be blessed."

One of my professors used to say that everything in the Bible before Genesis 12:1–3 leads up to it, and everything in the Bible after Genesis 12:1–3 fulfills it. There is a real sense in which that is true. In the promise we see the unfolding of God's sovereign plan of redemption, an unfolding that the apostle Paul will constantly cite as the product of Jesus' finished work, so that the promises of Abraham have come upon Gentiles who put their faith in Jesus Christ.

But in Genesis 12:1–3 we also see the flowering of world missions. "In you, all the families of the earth will be blessed." It is not only that Abraham is blessed, but that he is blessed in order to be a blessing to the nations. Joe Novenson says, "When God made his covenant promises with Abraham, Abraham went from being a guest on this planet, to a host."[8] Abraham had been a guest here until by grace he had been brought into God's redemptive plan. Afterward, no longer a guest, it was his role to be a blessing, just like a host is to be a blessing to his guest. Now he is a blessing to all the guests on this planet. It is a beautiful picture, and it goes right along with Isaac Watts's words from "How Sweet and Aweful Is the Place":

> Pity the nations, O Our God,
> Constrain the earth to come;
> Send thy victorious word abroad,
> And bring the strangers home.

Don't you love the beautiful way it talks about bringing the strangers home? Here is Abraham going from being a guest to a host, and now his job is to be a blessing to the nations. This is the foundation of world missions right here. You don't have to wait until Matthew 28:18–20.

We see the unfolding of Genesis 12 a few chapters later, as God comes to Abram and reiterates his promises to him. Many years have passed from Genesis 12 to Genesis 15, and during that time, the promises have not been fulfilled. It is from the context of Genesis 15:1–6 that Paul will say, "Then [Abram] believed God and it was credited to him as righteousness" (Rom. 4:3). And God also tells Abraham to "know for certain that your descendants will be strangers in a land that is not theirs, where they will be enslaved and oppressed four hundred years" (Gen. 15:13). So the seed promises are made to Abram again here as they were to Eve in Genesis 3:15.

Lo and behold when we turn forward to Exodus 2, we find the people of God crying out in the Old Testament under the burden of slavery in Egypt, and we read, "So God heard their groaning; and God remembered His covenant with Abraham, Isaac, and Jacob. God saw the sons of Israel and God took notice of them" (2:24). There is really just one story going on from Eve to Abraham to the exodus—a story that carries on even to the story of David.[9]

Psalm 78 reveals how 2 Samuel 7 fits in with Abraham and with the exodus. The psalmist tells us that David's reign is directly connected to God's purposes to advance the redemptive story despite the failure of the people of God under the leadership of Moses and the judges. According to Psalm 78—from Eve to Abraham to Moses to David—it is all one story, which God is working out.

Then, of course, the great passages that we have already noted in Jeremiah 31 and in Ezekiel 37 push forward the day when the Messiah will come and establish a new covenant, which will not be broken like the previous one. And it is so significant that as far as it is recorded in the Gospels, Jesus never, in his public ministry, appeals to those Jeremiah words about the new covenant; but on the night of his betrayal at his last Passover supper with his disciples, as he is instituting the covenant meal of the people of God for the ages to come and explaining the meaning and nature of his death, he will say, "This cup which is poured out for you is the new covenant in My blood" (Luke 22:20). We have a difficult time imagining what the disciples were able to comprehend. For six hundred years the people of God had been waiting in hope to see the new covenant promises of God established, and here was Jesus standing before his disciples announcing that the next day he would inaugurate the promises, but he emphasized that this covenant would be inaugurated by his own blood.

All of this makes sense, then, in light of Jesus' words to those two conflicted disciples on the road to Emmaus, words which meant, "Did you not know from the prophets how the Christ must suffer? Because this one redemptive plan of God is going to

---

[9] Review 2 Samuel 7:12–16.

be accomplished through my humiliation, my abasement, my cru-
cifixion, my burial, my death, my resurrection, my ascension, and
my rule at the right hand—but these will come through the valley
of humiliation." Never fail, in preaching the Old Testament, to
carry out those strands to the New Testament fulfillment, and do
not fail to connect the fulfillments to their Old Testament precur-
sors as you preach through the New Testament. It ties together
the whole redemptive plan of God and helps the people of God
make sense of the whole of Scripture.

5) Preach Grace from the Old Testament

Paul said to Timothy, "From childhood you have known the sacred
writings [Old Testament Scriptures] which are able to give you
the wisdom that leads to salvation through faith which is in Christ
Jesus" (2 Tim. 3:15). It is the Old Testament, the apostle Paul
says, that is able to give you the wisdom that leads to salvation
through faith. Here in the Old Testament is *sola fide*. Therefore, we
ought not be surprised that when Paul wants to prove the doctrine of justification by grace alone through faith alone in Christ
alone, he goes to Genesis 15. If someone had asked the apostle
Paul, "Paul, are people saved in the old covenant like they are in
the new covenant, you know, by grace alone through faith alone
in Christ alone?" the apostle Paul would have said, "I don't understand the question. The only question is, are they still saved the
same way in the new covenant as they were in the old covenant?
Because when I want to show you that salvation is by grace alone
through faith alone in Christ alone, I go to the old covenant
Scriptures. I will start with Genesis 15, for example."

That is why you can preach grace from the Old Testament. You
can preach grace even when you are expounding the Decalogue. I
think we often begin a series on the Ten Commandments in the
wrong place; rather than beginning in Exodus 20, we probably
ought to start in Exodus 19, because Exodus 19 provides the whole

framework for everything that happens in the rest of the book. Once the children of Israel got to Sinai, we find them mostly there for the remainder of the Pentateuch. The context of where they are, why they are there, and what is happening is vitally important. One of the things we learn as we expound the book of Exodus is that God's people were saved to worship.

Although I'd been a professing Christian for at least a dozen years, I didn't realize until seminary that Moses was not trying to pull a trick on Pharaoh, when he said, "Let My people go that they may celebrate a feast to Me in the wilderness" (Exod. 5:1). I thought Moses was playing a trick on Pharaoh to get him to let the children of God go. But the demand is repeated so many times in the book of Exodus that clearly God is teaching us that he brought the Israelites out of bondage so that they might glorify and enjoy him forever—so that they might worship him. Worship is central to his purposes, not peripheral.

Notice Exodus 20 where this very thing is emphasized. "Then God spoke all these words, saying, 'I am the LORD your God, who brought you out of the land of Egypt, out of the house of slavery. You shall have no other gods before Me" (vv. 1–3). Now, isn't that interesting? "I am the LORD your God who brought you out of the land of Egypt, out of the house of slavery. You shall have no other gods before Me." Do you notice the gospel logic there? It is not, "Keep these commandments and I will bring you out of Egypt." "Keep these commandments and I will redeem you." It is, "I have redeemed you. Now keep these commandments. I have already brought you out of the land of Egypt, out of the house of slavery. Now be like Me." Gospel logic always has grace before law. Now in our fallen experience, law is always before grace because there is always something before grace, and that is sin, and there is something before sin, and that is law (because sin is defined by law and the breaking of it). That is how it is in our fallen experience: law, sin, grace. But in our salvation experience, in our redemptive experience, in our experience of sanctification, it is always grace before law. As we are expounding the law from Exodus 20, if we pay attention to the very framework of Exodus 19 and then the prologue, we will expound the law in light of God's redeeming grace.

But we can also preach grace from the Old Testament in a surprising way. Some of you have heard Ed Clowney's famous sermon on "David's Mighty Men."[10] David is speaking his last words, and as an old man often does, he reflects on the glory days of his life. He wants to tell the people about his mighty men. In 2 Samuel 23:13, he pauses. He started to name his mighty men, and it is almost like, "I can't just tell you the names of these men. I've got to tell you what these men were like. Let me just give you a taste of what these men were like."

> Then three of the thirty chief men went down and came to David in the harvest time to the cave of Adullam, while the troop of the Philistines was camping in the valley of Rephaim. David was then in the stronghold, while the garrison of the Philistines was then in Bethlehem. David had a craving and said, "Oh that someone would give me water to drink from the well of Bethlehem which is by the gate!" So the three mighty men broke through the camp of the Philistines, and drew water from the well of Bethlehem which was by the gate, and took it and brought it to David. Nevertheless he would not drink it, but poured it out to the LORD; and he said, "Be it far from me, O LORD, that I should do this. Shall I drink the blood of the men who went in jeopardy of their lives?" Therefore he would not drink it. These things the three mighty men did. (vv. 13–17)

He said, "Let me just tell you about these men. One day I am in the cave and I'm not asking anybody to do anything. I am just

---

[10] Edmund Clowney, "David's Mighty Men" (recalled by author as sermon preached on 2 Samuel 23:8–39, Covenant Theological Seminary, St. Louis, MO, c. 1985, chapel service).

speaking out loud. I am away from my hometown. There are filthy, uncircumcised Philistines in my hometown and there is nothing in the world that I would like more than to draw a cup of water from the well of my hometown, Bethlehem." And three of the mighty men heard David speaking to himself, and they said, "Let's do it." And maybe one of them said, "Look, that thing is ringed with Philistines. They've got sentinels several hundred yards from the scene. I mean, the well is at the gates of the city. There is no way." And the others responded, "Let's do it."

So these three men make their way across the desert. And they go to Bethlehem, and I don't know what they do. Do they fight their way in and fight their way out, and one draws while the others fight? I don't know how, but they get that water from the well of Bethlehem. And then maybe the hardest thing is coming back across the desert and not drinking that water.

And they get to David and they say, "Hmm, David, we got some water from Bethlehem for you." And David pours it out on the ground. I would have coldcocked him right then. But you see what David is saying: "I'm not worthy of this kind of devotion. I don't deserve men who will risk their lives, showing that kind of devotion, that kind of loyalty, that kind of covenant fidelity to me. I don't deserve that." And then Clowney goes on to read the names of the rest of the mighty men, the last of which is Uriah the Hittite (v. 39).

Did you know that Uriah the Hittite was one of David's mighty men?

And then Clowney asks this question: "Did David show Uriah devotion and loyalty and faithfulness and covenant love and fidelity?" He takes you back to 2 Samuel 11 and shows you the immense betrayal of Uriah by David. He then asks you to turn to Psalm 51 and says, "You know, after David's colossal failure, this lack of covenant faithfulness, covenant loyalty, this failure of *chesed*, of lovingkindness toward Uriah, a man who was among his mighty men who showed such devotion and loyalty and *chesed* and covenant faithfulness and love to David, on what basis could David (or anyone else) dare hope for forgiveness?"

Well, after this immense and unmitigated failure, Nathan confronts David. What in the world does David say to God? There are so many today who, tragically, want to teach their people to plead their own covenant faithfulness to God as the basis of their perseverance. But I want you to see what David says in Psalm 51. "Be gracious to me, O God, according to [Your *chesed*,] Your lovingkindness [Your devotion, Your covenant love, Your covenant fidelity]" (v. 1). David knows that he cannot flee to his own faithfulness for refuge from just judgment, because he has been unfaithful in the extreme.

In fact, he has not only been unfaithful towards Uriah, but he tells us in this psalm, "Against You, You only, I have sinned" (v. 4). He has been unfaithful to God. His covenant faithfulness is a filthy rag. Only the *chesed*, only the lovingkindness, only the covenant love and loyalty and fidelity of God can save him. He well understood that he needed the costly and free grace of God, the undeserved and unmerited grace of God.

Brothers, preach grace from the Old Testament.

A friend of mine graduated from the Naval Academy many years ago. He came to faith in Christ there at the Naval Academy through the faithful gospel witness of some Navigators. He bounced around in different Bible churches over the years, and he said to me that after being a Christian for twelve years, he came to a church one night where he heard grace preached naturally and exegetically from the Old Testament. He turned to his wife, Jeannie, and he said, "Jeannie, we are home," because he had heard the grace of God and saving faith in Christ preached from the Old Testament.

It's my prayer that hundreds and hundreds and thousands and thousands of Christians will be able to say that of your churches.

"We came to this church, and we heard the grace of God preached expositionally from the Old Testament, and we were home."

6) Preach the Character of God from the Old Testament

If you want a model for how to preach the character of God from the Old Testament, just listen to everything that you can get your hands on by R. C. Sproul. Have you ever heard his sermon on Dagon?[11] Go listen to it. The Old Testament is our primary source for knowledge of many biblical doctrines, and one of those doctrines is the attributes of God. The Old Testament is far fuller in its explication and elaboration on the attributes of God in many ways than the New Testament. One of the grave dangers in neglecting the Old Testament is that we will produce a generation of Christians gravely deficient in the knowledge of these fundamental matters.

Consider what we learn about God from 2 Samuel 7. It is right in the context of that Davidic covenant. But look at how it starts: David wants to build a temple for the Lord. He is dwelling in a cedar-lined palace, and he looks over at the ark of the covenant of God—the visible symbol and manifestation of the presence of God with his people in the old covenant—and it is in a tent. It is a glorious tent. It is a relatively big tent for a nomad. It's an ornate tent, but it's a tent. And David says, "It's not right for me to live in a palace while the ark of God is in a tent." And his humility moves him to say, "Lord God, I want to build a temple for you that is greater than the palace that I live in. It's not right that I live in something more glorious than what the ark of God is housed in."

God sends Nathan to David to say, "Are you going to be the one who will build me a house to dwell in?" And notice what God says: "For I have not dwelt in a house since the day I brought up the sons of Israel from Egypt, even to this day; but I have been

---

[11] R. C. Sproul, "Not a Chance" (sermon preached on 1 Sam. 6:1–14, available through Ligonier Ministries).

moving about in a tent, even in a tabernacle. Wherever I have gone with all the sons of Israel, did I speak a word with one of the tribes of Israel, which I commanded to shepherd My people Israel, saying, 'Why have you not built Me a house of cedar?'" (2 Sam. 7:6–7).

That's a glorious passage about the character of God. Do you know what it tells us? It tells us that this majestic, awesome, transcendent, creating, redeeming God is humble. In effect he says, "David, I want to tell you something. When my people were going through the wilderness, living in tents, I lived in a tent with them—right in the middle of it—and I never asked them to do anything for me, other than to let me live with them right where they were."

What does this tell you about the character of God? It is the same thing that tells us: "The Word became flesh, and dwelt among us, and we saw His glory" (John 1:14). But it was the Father who had revealed that part of himself in the old covenant.

7) Preach Experientially from the Old Testament

John Calvin and the Puritans all emphasized that the Psalms give us the language of Christian experience. The greatest transaction in the history of humanity is the transaction that occurs on the cross of Christ recorded for us in Matthew 27:46 when the Lord Jesus Christ himself cries out, "My God, My God, why have You forsaken Me?" It is the greatest expression of experience in the history of this world, and it is drawn from Psalm 22.

Don't belittle the powerful, eternally valuable, currently applicable, experiential teaching that we get from the Old Testament—from the Psalms, from Jeremiah, from Isaiah, from Job. When we are preaching a funeral, how often do we call to mind the words of Job, "The LORD gave and the LORD has taken away. Blessed be the name of the LORD" (Job 1:21).

How often do the people of God want to hear the Twenty-third Psalm read to them in the hour of their death or the death of their loved ones? Don't you love the way that Isaac Watts renders that last line, "There would I find a settled rest, while others go and come; no more a stranger, nor a guest, but like a child at home."[12] It is that language of experience that supplies to us the language and the framework for Christian experience, even today. And that experience is wonderful and varied and deep and includes great anguish and desperation and pain from time to time, which stands in contrast to the shallow, superficial, slap-happy spirituality that pervades the evangelical culture today.

Those great theologians of our age such as Steely Dan, who once sang, "They got a name for the winners in the world. I want a name when I lose. They call Alabama the 'Crimson Tide.' Call me 'Deacon Blues.'"[13] Steely Dan wanted a song to sing when hearts are broken. Where do Christians find that? In the Psalms. The Psalms give you words to sing when your heart is broken. Preach experientially from the Old Testament.

The great bulk of biblical teaching on the subjective and experiential side of Christianity is to be found in the Old Testament, and it is there especially in Psalms and Job and Jeremiah. We see Christian experience and emotion reflected in their inner moods, their struggles, which are our inner moods and our struggles, and to ignore this vein of revelation will lead inevitably either to superficial religion or to a blank incomprehension when we find God trying our faith.

8) Preach the Christian Life from the Old Testament

Very often as people urge us to preach redemptive historically and to preach christologically, they make fun of what they call exemplaristic or moralistic preaching. They say, "The Old Testament wasn't given as a how-to guide for the Christian life. You are not to learn how to be a godly man from the story of Joseph. It is all about christology and redemptive history. You are not to learn

---

[12] Isaac Watts, "My Shepherd Will Supply My Need" (1719).
[13] Steely Dan, "Deacon Blues" from the album *Aja* (1977).

moralistic messages and principles from these events, to pound the people of God with these lessons today."

Now the problem with that assertion is it goes directly contrary to Jesus and Paul. Jesus will say, "Remember Lot's wife" (Luke 17:32). And the apostle Paul will say, "Now these things happened [he has just talked about the Exodus, crossing of the Red Sea] as examples for us, so that we would not crave evil things as they also craved" (1 Cor. 10:6). Someone needs to clue Paul in that he has a problem with moralistic teaching of the Old Testament, because Paul, happily, will take an Old Testament passage chock full of redemptive, historical, and christological significance and still see moral exhortation for Christians.

This is a reminder of our obligation and responsibility, too. We are not to shrink from moral exhortation in our preaching of the Bible, whether from the Old Testament or New, because the preachers of the Old Testament and New, under divine inspiration, do not shrink from bringing the imperatives of God's Word onto the hearts and lives of believers. Yes, the Christian life is based on the work of Christ, the power of the gospel, and the grace of the Holy Spirit. Yes, we need God's grace in sanctification as much as justification. Yes, we need, as Chalmers so forcefully preached, "the expulsive power of a new affection," if we are to join the battle against indwelling sin. But grace has its own imperatives, and the gospel does not hesitate to call us to response and responsibility.

If we are going to be faithful to God's Word, we are going to preach the Christian life to Christians from the Old Testament (as well as the New); we will understand and fully appreciate the glorious new covenant aspects of the doctrine of sanctification; we will not try to anachronistically read them back into the old covenant text. But when applying the old covenant text to new covenant believers, we will not fail to bring its moral exhortation to bear on their hearts and lives, in light of the glorious new covenant realities of which they blessedly partake.

CHAPTER 3

PREACHING WITH THE CULTURE IN VIEW

R. Albert Mohler Jr.

A ddressing a topic like "preaching with the culture in view" is necessarily something of a dangerous business. That is because there are perils on both sides of the issue, a polarity of dangers into which people can easily fall. On the one hand, there are some who look at culture with no seriousness at all; they ignore the obvious and try to—or at least they *claim* to try to—disengage from culture entirely. Many people today are convinced that culture is irrelevant to our preaching. But it is not, and a simple look around our homes and offices should be enough to convince us of that fact. Even as Christians, we are deeply imbedded in a culture. We use a language that is common to us, and that language is a product of culture. We meet in comfortable buildings. There is electricity that gives us light. All of these things make sense to us, and we are comfortable with them. Yet most Christians throughout the history of the church have no connection to these things, which we take for granted. They have no experience with all the things that frame and shape our perspective much more than we would often allow ourselves to recognize.

On the other hand, there are those who allow the culture to

become dominant in their ministries, for the culture becomes such a fascination for them that they are themselves representatives of an inculturated ministry. The cultural captivity of the church is always a danger. Both of these tendencies are perilous errors of which every preacher should be aware.

Preaching with the Culture in View

The best way to approach the topic of "preaching with the culture in view" is to begin with preaching itself, especially expository preaching. I define expository preaching as that mode of Christian preaching which takes as its central purpose the presentation and application of the text of the Bible. All other issues and concerns are subordinated to the central task of presenting the biblical text. As the Word of God, the text of Scripture has the right to establish both the substance and the structure of the sermon. Genuine exposition takes place when the preacher sets forth the meaning and message of the biblical text and makes clear how the Word of God establishes the identity and worldview of the church as the people of God.

The first thing that must be said about preaching with the culture in view is that our primary attention as preachers is not to the culture at all but to the text of Scripture. The most important part of our role as preachers is that we be scholars of Scripture. Thus we start with a definition of preaching that directs us above all to the text of Scripture. Every other issue and every other concern is secondary to that one central task of presenting the biblical text.

That means that we are to present that text in the way the apostles would have presented it. We are to present it in its enduring and eternal truthfulness, understanding that the truth of that text is unchanged and unchanging even as its authority also is unchanged and unchanging. Yet even as we do this, we must also make clear how the Word of God establishes the identity and worldview of the church as the people of God, and in the process of doing so we will find ourselves unavoidably linking the Word of God and applying the Word of God to the culture in which we live, the culture which in so many ways shapes the experience of the people to whom we minister.

The church of the Lord Jesus Christ starts from a very different place than other people in talking about the culture. That's because we are not talking primarily about cultural transformation or cultural renewal or cultural recovery; we are talking above all about preaching the gospel to sinners. That is a very different vantage point from anyone else's in the world. We are concerned for the culture because that is where we find those sinners; our concern is not ultimately for the culture itself. Everything we see around us is passing, including culture. The task of the church is to reach persons from every tongue and tribe and people and nation who are each themselves deeply imbedded in a symbolic and cultural system of meaning.

Yet even in the face of cultural diversity, Christians must assert the transcultural authority of the Bible, because they are the only people on the entire planet with a message that is addressed to persons within every culture. Moreover, we have the only message that does not have to be transformed and redefined in every cultural circumstance, because we are talking about constants like sin, the character of God, and the cross of the Lord Jesus Christ. We begin with the primacy of the text of Scripture, because we begin with certain definite convictions about that text that hold true in every culture—its inerrancy, its authority, and its total trustworthiness.

In one sense, all we have to do is put culture in its place. That is a difficult task, because even as there are polarities—some who give too much attention to the culture and others who give it inadequate attention—we must understand that we all swing between different seasons in our personal experience. Throughout the history of the church, Christians have swung between seasons of engagement and seasons of withdrawal. In fact, Christians seeking to be faithful in every generation have had to respond in different ways to the cultural realities confronting them.

The official United Nations definition of a culture is this: "A set of distinctive spiritual, material, intellectual, and emotional features of society or a social group, which encompasses, in addition to art and literature, lifestyle, ways of living together, value systems, traditions, and beliefs." Here is a definition of culture offered by anthropologists: "The system of shared beliefs, values, customs, behaviors, and artifacts that the members of society use to cope with this world and with one another, and that are transmitted from generation to generation through learning." That definition probably is a little bit more helpful. Culture is that which allows human beings to relate to one another. We must have certain tools like language. We must live within a system of meaning that allows us to communicate with one another, understand one another, and eventually even to trust one another so we can live as neighbors with one another.

In reality, however, there is no definition of culture that proves sufficient, no description that is comprehensive enough, because culture encompasses everything about our experience, our knowledge, our thinking, and our memory. In fact, we are a bit like Aristotle's fish. The philosopher Aristotle told a parable of a fish in which he asked the question, "If you want to know what being wet feels like, whom do you ask?" His answer is one that is both surprising and obvious at the same time. The last creature you should ask about being wet is a fish, because he has no idea that he *is* wet. He has no point of reference, having never been dry. That is the way we are when it comes to culture. We are like fish in that we are not even able to recognize where our culture is influencing us. From the time we were in the crib, culture has been shaping our hopes, our perspectives, our systems of meaning and interpretation, and even our intellectual tools.

This has been particularly dangerous for evangelicals in America, because we just assume that what we experience is normal and that becomes blinding for us. If we assume, for instance, that the early church had any connection to the kind of life we lead and the conveniences we take for granted, then we would be badly mistaken. If we assume they shared our understanding of human freedom and autonomy, which has risen from our political system, or the sense of security that most of us possess in most moments of our lives, then we would be wrong. And the problem becomes even more acute if we think about God's people in the Old Testament. The American evangelical movement emerged primarily in the years after World War II, when America's culture was, in the minds of most evangelical leaders, a friendly context for the emergence of a conservative Christian movement. Evangelicals felt very much at home in America during this period, and they saw the world's problems as being mostly abroad. Nazism had been primarily a European problem, and even the most pressing objects of cultural concern emerging in their own day—Communism, Marxism, liberal theology—they saw as imports from Europe. Of course they recognized regional differences such as those between rural and urban areas, and Northern and Southern people. But still they did not think of the culture as being inherently hostile.

Niebuhr's Treatment of Christ and Culture

During this time, the most sophisticated attempts to understand culture and its meaning came from mainline Protestantism. In 1949 H. Richard Niebuhr delivered a series of lectures at Austin Presbyterian Seminary in Texas, which were later published as *Christ and Culture*.[1] In those lectures, Niebuhr offered a typological scheme of how Christ, or Christ's church, is related to culture. In

---

[1] H. Richard Niebuhr, *Christ and Culture* (New York: Harper Perennial, 1956).

time, Niebuhr's typology became fixed in the Protestant imagination, and it is a useful place to start in thinking about the question.

Niebuhr's first type was *Christ against culture*, in which the world is understood to be under the domain of evil and darkness, and the church is seen as the kingdom, a new society. For those who saw Christ and culture in these terms, faithful Christian living necessitated a complete withdrawal from the culture. As an example of this, Niebuhr pointed to Leo Tolstoy, and we might also look at examples such as the Old Order Amish or the Mennonites, who live apart from culture. Of course, the problem with this is that it does not work. You cannot withdraw, not totally. You can withdraw from certain sectors of the society, but no one is going to give up the society's language, for example. Christians do not have a distinctive language; we do not have a Christian lingua franca. In fact, it is to God's glory that we anticipate seeing believers from every tongue and tribe and people and nation standing before God's throne, declaring his glory in different languages.

Even the Amish and the Mennonites cannot withdraw entirely. A story is told of the late Senator Daniel Patrick Moynihan of New York, who was visiting one of the Old Order Amish communities that abound in Upstate New York. As the senator was talking with the Amish people, one man indicated that he was having some trouble with one of his daughters. "My daughter," the man said, "is being influenced by Catholicism."

Telling this story later, Moynihan, himself a Roman Catholic, said, "I knew we were good, but I didn't know we were this good." Nonetheless, he asked the father, "Just how is this showing up in your daughter?"

The Amish father answered, "Well, I heard her talking to some of her friends, and she's been talking about Madonna." This Amish father's problem is a lot deeper than he knows!

One of the other reasons the Amish have not been completely able to withdraw is that they want to sell milk. I do not intend at all to ridicule the Amish. Their efforts are in many ways well intended to try to show their commitment to Christ. But the Amish do not use technology in any form. In Amish homes there is no electricity or telephone, and there are no modern conveniences. But there are such conveniences in an Amish *barn*, because the state regulatory agencies require that milk be produced under certain defined circumstances, and Occupational Safety and Health Administration (OSHA) regulations require that there be a phone to call for help. All this is to say that it is impossible to completely withdraw from any culture. Even as we seek to live the Christian life, we are deeply imbedded in culture.

Niebuhr's second type was the *Christ of culture*. This is the opposite of the first; it is an acculturated Christianity. Those who are inclined toward this model see no distinction between the church and the culture. In fact, they see an identification of the one with the other. There have been occurrences of explicit experiments in combining the church and the culture, blurring the distinction between the two. There have also been times when the combination of church and culture was more of an accumulated cultural reality, such as the culture of Victorian England, or in many ways, the culture of nineteenth-century Protestantism in Germany. In this model Christ is understood to make no counter-cultural claims upon his people. Christianity is understood to be culturally accessible. The church and the culture are synonymous. The problem with this ought to be painfully obvious. If we cannot see a distinction between the church and the world, we are simply not able to read the New Testament.

Niebuhr's third type or model was *Christ above culture*, the synthesis of the preceding two. Niebuhr believed this was the dominant understanding of Christianity through the first nineteen centuries of the church's history. This is a middle way, and it calls for neither withdrawal nor abdication. Christ and the culture are both understood to make claims upon citizens, and the claim is that these can be negotiated. There are tensions, but they are resolvable, and the church negotiates its way through the competing demands, all the while avoiding extremes. This is an exhortation we hear regularly today: *Let's negotiate the culture, and let's avoid appearing extreme.* Of course Christ makes claims upon the church that go beyond anything the culture will understand, but let's be really careful how we let that secret out.

The fourth model was *Christ and culture in paradox.* These are the true dualists, who see Christ and culture not only as distinct but as two completely separate realms with no point of contact or meaning and with no synthesis possible. Perhaps the greatest example of this idea Niebuhr could have offered was Martin Luther's theology of the two kingdoms. But of course, that cannot work either, because we would find ourselves continually going back and forth. We are not bifurcated people. We cannot live compartmentalized lives. We are not just citizens at one moment and Christians the next. Christ makes a total claim upon everything that we are. We cannot live with such a paradox, and we cannot accept a dualism like this. All human effort is hopelessly mired in godlessness. If you hold to this paradox position, you believe there is an ethic of the world and an ethic of the church, and the two are mutually exclusive. Thus, you simply walk from one to the other. When you are operating in this world, you play by this world's rules. But when you are in the other world, you play by its rules. This leads, Niebuhr said, to antinomianism and to cultural conservatism.

Niebuhr's fifth model is where he seems to be pointing us, that is, to *Christ the transformer of culture.* These are the conversionists, and they are far more hopeful than the dualists. They understand the distinction between Christ and the culture, but they also understand that it is the mission of the church to transform the culture with the claims of Christ. We continually hear this kind of language: "Let's go out and redeem the culture. Let's go out and conquer the culture in the name of Christ. Let's transform every dimension of the culture, whether the media and the arts, or business and finance, and let's subdue them to the claims of Christ. Let's have a more Christian military and a more Christian economy and a more Christian realm of arts." This leads to a very progressive impulse, one which looks to a better world and a better condition if we will only do this. It promises transformation, hopes for cultural redemption, and leads to Christian activism.

The interesting thing is that when Niebuhr gets to the end of his typology, it appears that he loses nerve. Instead of clearly advocating this last option—Christ transforming culture—as the one the church must take, he seems to withdraw and say there really is no right answer. But if that is the case, then what are we to take from all of this? I want to suggest that in fact there is no right answer; there is no answer that will prove right for all Christians, in all times, and under all circumstances. If you read the history of the church, or if you read the Scripture, you'll discover that God's people in different times have had to respond to the culture in very different ways. For example, you would have to engage the culture quite differently if you were a captive in Babylon rather than a resident in the kingdom of Israel or Jerusalem in the southern kingdom. You would have to engage the culture differently if you were living in a time of explicit oppression—when Christians were being chased into the catacombs of Rome, for example—rather than in Victorian England, when the royal family had its own designated priests. Even in our own times, the believing church has been confronted by realities that have forced us to rethink all this. We thought we had an answer to this problem of Christ and culture, but now we find ourselves in a very different situation facing very different challenges.

One danger of which we should be aware when we think about these issues is the myth of the Golden Age, the myth of nostalgia. "If only we could return to some previous moment," some people say. This is a false promise, and we need to be very clear about that. For instance, there are some evangelicals who would like to go back to an era like the 1950s, when everyone knew that marriage is between one man and one woman, and that a fetus is a living human being. No one worried about the elementary school teacher changing genders over the weekend. The past sounds nice, but we must remember that to return to that time is also to return to an era when African-Americans could not vote and were denied basic civil rights. The reality is that there is no Golden Era. At every moment we have to see that the culture is as fallen as the human beings who comprise it.

So given Niebuhr's typology, how ought Christians to think through culture? What does it mean to preach with the culture in view? First of all, culture cannot be meaningless. We are charged to think through this theologically, and the reason we have to think about this is that our people—the ones to whom we preach, the ones to whom we seek to proclaim the gospel—are deeply immersed in it. Thus, we have to do some very deep cultural analysis in order to make sure we are even communicating with them. Culture cannot be meaningless, but it cannot be our main concern either. It cannot be the primary focus of our thought because it is passing.

Augustine's Two Cities

Thankfully, we are not the first generation of Christians to try to think through these questions. In order to gain a more cogent understanding of how we should understand the culture, we need to go back much further than Richard Niebuhr. We must at least go back to Augustine and his work *The City of God*, in which he tried to apply the Word of God to his situation—a time when all the cultural questions were coming in an acute and unavoidable way. When Rome was falling, people could not avoid talking about the culture. They could not avoid talking about the symbolic sys-

tem of meaning that held everything together, because Rome had
been that symbolic system of meaning for the inhabitants of
Augustine's world. But Augustine was a Christian pastor, and he
bore responsibility to teach his people from the Word of God.
Thus, when he wrote his book *The City of God*, he was trying to
teach his people how they should understand the demands of
Christ and the realities of culture even in a time of emergency and
urgency and collapse.

Augustine spoke of two cities, the heavenly city and the earthly
city—the City of God and the City of Man. He defined these two
cities in terms of two different loves, two different ambitions, two
different passions, and two different allegiances. I believe this is the
most helpful conceptual understanding of the relation between
Christ and culture in the history of the Christian church. Augustine
thought this through theologically and biblically, and so offered
more than a sociological analysis of Rome's fall. He was not merely
trying to defend Christians against the claim that Christianity had
weakened the empire, even though in one sense it obviously had
done so, for the moment one declares that Jesus is Lord rather than
Caesar, imperial ambitions are weakened.

Augustine understood that there is only one city that is eternal—the City of God. The earthly city is passing. So Augustine asks
his people why they had ever thought otherwise. Why have we
allowed ourselves to be fooled into thinking that Rome is eternal?
Throughout the annals of human history, empires rise and fall.
None survive forever. Augustine was speaking and preaching to
Christians, and he reminded his listeners that we who are believers,
God's people saved by the blood of the Lamb—God's claimed and
chosen people—are citizens of the city of heaven. We do not live
there yet, but our citizenship there is more real than our citizenship here. In the City of God, there is only one love, and that is
the love of God. It is undiluted and undeflected, and it is maximized
to an infinite degree because the only residents of this city will be

those who have been glorified and who see no longer through a dark glass. There will be no other loves, no struggle to manage one's heart. Isn't that a great promise? There will be no struggle in the heavenly city to manage one's passions. There will be only one passion, only one allegiance, only one thought. And as Augustine understood, there will be no Romans in heaven. There will be no Americans in heaven, either—only sinners saved by grace.

Therefore, Augustine argued, it is the Christian's responsibility to think of the City of Man only through his citizenship in the City of God. This is extremely important. We do not care about the culture for the culture's sake. Our concern for the culture is simply because that is where the sinners are, with whom we will share the gospel, to whom we will preach the gospel, and with whom we live as neighbors.

When Augustine said that our primary citizenship is in the heavenly city, he was only following Paul, who wrote in Philippians 3:20, "But our citizenship is in heaven, and from it we await a Savior, the Lord Jesus Christ." And yet we are not there in heaven yet. In this life, which is not an accident but rather God's purpose for us, we are deeply imbedded in the City of Man. So Augustine asked, what then are we to do since we are citizens of the heavenly city, yet living in the earthly city? What should we do? Do we ignore it? Withdraw from it? Scandalize it? Reject it? Do we just embrace it? Not according to Augustine, who argued that we ought to love those who are in the city while not loving the city itself. We cannot love the city, but we must love those who are in the city because they are the objects of God's love. So that is what we do, just as Jesus commanded. "Which is the greatest commandment in the Law?" Jesus was asked. And his answer was: "You shall love the Lord your God with all your heart and with all your soul and with all your mind. . . . And a second is like it: You shall love your neighbor as yourself. On these two commandments depend all the Law and the Prophets" (Matt. 22:36–40). Jesus made very clear that love of neighbor is derivative of love of God. And so we really cannot say that we love God if we do not love our neighbor.

Augustine then tried to apply that commandment pastorally, saying that the City of Man is falling, passing away, and yet it is filled with people whose passions are for that city. The City of Man is populated by people who want to find their deepest meaning and deepest satisfactions in this city, and yet they will never find it there. Thus, Augustine said we should not be surprised that sinners act like sinners. We should not be surprised when we see sinners sinning, institutionalizing their sin, celebrating their sin. And we cannot withdraw from sinful people, because we know they are the objects of God's love.

The Christian's Dual Citizenship

In some sense, the Christian does hold a dual citizenship. However, we must be very careful not to commit the error of making those citizenships equal to one another. One of them is passing, and the other is eternal. Or put another way: one is missiological, and the other is doxological. The only reason we are here is to show the glory of God in the preaching of the gospel, in the formation of local churches that will display God's glory in a fallen world, and in preaching the gospel until he comes. There is no other purpose for the continuation of culture. There is no other purpose for the continuation of this earthly life but that God's glory would be seen in the preaching of the gospel, in the gathering of the nations, and in the display of his glory in faithful congregations living out the gospel before a fallen world.

When the apostle Paul said that our citizenship is in heaven, he did not deny that there is an earthly citizenship that is also a matter of our accountability as disciples. This is the same apostle, after all, who invoked his Roman citizenship, and who made very clear in Romans 13 that God's people have an obligation to civil society and to civil government. This is because culture is not an accident. It is not a mere sociological development. No, one of God's gifts to all peoples is that we would know an institution like marriage, that we would be able to constrain sin to some degree by the presence of government and law, and that we would show God's glory in the punishing of the evildoer, the upholding of justice, and the vindication of the innocent. This is one of the constants that we often do not understand. God's glory is seen when even a pagan judge rules rightly, because there is an accidental testimony to God's law and to God's character even there. The same thing is true—God's glory is seen and there is a witness to the Creator's grace—when two unbelievers are married to each other and maintain that marriage in covenant fidelity. They may not know it, but they are testifying to God's glory and rule by their very following of this call of common grace.

Moreover, we should see culture as a gift so that we can communicate. God has given gifts to his people—gifts of artistic ability, gifts of musical ability, gifts of linguistic and literary ability. We should be thankful that there are people who know how to design buildings. We should be thankful that engineering and architecture have constructed a place where we can meet, work, and play safely. We should also be thankful that we can gather together without the threat of gangs bursting into the room and dispersing our meeting. We should be thankful that we can look at testimonies to the glory of God in some of the most beautiful artistic expressions ever made. We sing music, and this music is a representation of a cultural language we have learned. The words of our songs as linguistic units are still a part of that culture, but by God's grace they are able to convey God's eternal truth revealed to us out of his Word.

Yet for all this, we must always keep culture at a distance. We can never give it our full allegiance. For the sake of the people of God, we must instruct them continuously to remember that their citizenship is in heaven. Here is the danger if we do not: we are living in a culture that makes it very easy for Christians to believe that our citizenship is, in a very meaningful way, right here, when the New Testament excludes that as a Christian option.

Some Christians may be tempted to feel right at home in our culture. However, our culture presents some very significant interpretive problems for the Christian gospel. How can we possibly communicate the gospel to people whose conceptual system, which they have derived from this cultural context, comes with a complete set of assumptions and passions and allegiances that may make the hearing of the gospel more complex than we might think? In the last two centuries, and especially in recent years, there have been massive shifts in the Western cultural framework. Human society in the West has been transformed with the rise of modernity and industrialization. Indeed, Henry Adams was right when he said, writing in 1905, that a boy born in 1890 would have more in common with a boy born in the time of Moses than he would with a boy born in just the first years of the twentieth century.

Social and cultural change is happening at such a rapid pace that we now assume it. We assume that things change—in a progressive direction—and we assume that things are, as one postmodern analyst said, always liquid. For human beings living in previous eras, of course, it was not that way at all. In earlier generations, most people assumed that their great-grandchildren would someday inherit a world very much like their own. We are in a very different time. In the twentieth century, we have had the rise of urbanization, the spread of technology, the availability of transportation, and access to communication. We have gone from making products to becoming what Robert Reich calls "symbolic analysts."[2] Most Americans in the twenty-first century will work in occupations in which they analyze symbols. That may not be their

---

[2] Robert B. Reich, *The Work of Nations* (New York: Vintage, 1991), 177–80.

title, but that is what they are doing. They are dealing with ideas. They are "knowledge workers," as Peter Drucker calls them.[3] Most of us do not do much with our hands anymore, and it shows. We do not know how to fix things. But who cares? We do not fix things anyway; we just throw them away and get new ones. All these cultural assumptions are just very strange in light of human history, and yet they are the assumptions and values that permeate our people's thoughts, emotions, and intellectual frameworks.

Understanding Our Cultural Context

Here is the reality: the importance of culture generally comes to evangelical Christians when we think of missions somewhere else. We have inherited something of a *National Geographic* understanding of the importance of culture. We know it is important "over there," and so we look at how people in other places dress, and we look at their language and system, and we tell ourselves that what they do, and how they speak, and how they act is not normal. *We* are normal. The fact is, however, we need to turn that same perspective back on ourselves. If we are unaware of the missiological challenges of this culture, we blind ourselves to the obvious. Therefore, I want to discuss just a few facets of our culture that might help us to understand where we are missiologically. Any list like this is necessarily reductionistic and perspectival, but perhaps these thoughts will help us to understand a bit better the cultural system that influences where our church members are and where lost persons are. It is worth noting that each of these points begins with the word *self*, which says something about our cultural context.

The first is *self-fulfillment*. We live in a culture focused on self-fulfillment, on radical individualism. Most Americans believe that life is something of a quest and that the self is something of a pro-

---

[3] First used in Drucker's *Landmarks of Tomorrow* (New York: Harper, 1959).

ject. And in this project of self-fulfillment, they believe that what is most important in life is the ability to develop an exciting, exhilarating, satisfying, and secure sense of self. They look for fulfillment primarily within the self. The self becomes the only unit of experience, and the reference of all meaning is the solitary self which engages other selves only insofar as it chooses. This comes with the therapeutic revolution, as Philip Rieff said in his book, *The Triumph of the Therapeutic*. We are now living in an age in which the primary question asked by most persons is, *Am I well?* What they mean is, *Am I well?* in a psychological sense. Of course, this has now become so ubiquitous in this society that the psychotherapeutic worldview suggests that all Americans, all human beings throughout all history, in fact, are either in therapy or in denial.

Therapeutic modalities and answering questions with a therapeutic response have become the reflex of our society. If you doubt this, just go into your local Christian bookstore; what you are likely to find are rows upon rows of books that demonstrate this very therapeutic worldview, with just a few Bible verses added to make it *Christian*. We have to understand that for Americans this is normal. It is normal to be told that the self is the center of the meaning system, and that the self is a project that they undertake throughout the entirety of their lives. As a result, most Americans believe that their major problem is something that has happened to them, and that their solution is to be found within. In other words, they believe that they have an *alien problem* that is to be resolved with an *inner solution*. What the gospel says, however, is that we have an *inner problem* that demands an *alien solution*—a righteousness that is not our own. Once we begin to understand how that dichotomy comes together, we can see better how we can think we are talking about the gospel, yet people in this culture will hear it as merely a new form of therapy.

The second facet of our culture is *self-sufficiency*. People in our society are very much prone to believe that every individual possesses whatever is needed for fulfillment and meaning, that it lies deep within, and that all we need to do is call it out. We are the self-sufficient cause of all meaning and happiness, and furthermore, we are our self-sufficient authority as well. There is no external authority, there is no hierarchy, and there is no need for tradition or custom or manner. We can redefine ourselves, and we are sufficient to remake ourselves in any way we may see fit. This self-sufficiency is buttressed by the society, which tends to reward those who appear to be most successfully self-sufficient, rather than those who understand their categorical insufficiency. Again, this has a great deal to do with how the gospel is heard. The gospel is not about how we can become more self-sufficient. The very fact that the term begins with the word *self* is a contradiction of the gospel, but it is a cultural assumption.

The third facet is *self-definition*, an issue that has become radically more important in recent years, because it is perhaps the extension of some of these other cultural movements. Most Americans now believe that we have the ability to define ourselves. This is pushing the limits of autonomy. We will now define what it means to be human. We will define what it means to be male and female. We will define what it means to be able to change those categories. We will define how we should be ordered together, and we will even redefine marriage. We are self-defining, and we will claim for ourselves the right to define humanity, gender, marriage, and sexuality. We will define authority and everything else as well. All this reaches its apex in those who are suggesting that what we now need to do is control our evolution. This is the new argument coming from many of the radical evolutionary theorists: we need to control our evolution by using these new technologies in order to redefine what it means to be human. And of course this comes hand in hand with postmodern theories of truth, which become intellectual conveniences for this process of self-definition. One simply argues that all truth is socially constructed and denies that truth is in any way objective and can be communicated in sentences or in propositions; and one simply says there are no fixed truths or fixed definitions or fixed authorities. Thus, we can define ourselves however we wish.

The next characteristic of our culture is *self-absorption*, the centrality of the project of the self. This has led to such things as what Barbara Dafoe Whitehead calls "expressive divorce." Americans have become so self-absorbed that you will find many people now saying, "I divorced because I needed to in order to become the self that I need to be." So you have people talking about how this became a learning experience for them, one more forward step in the project of the self. Of course, no one would have talked like that even twenty or thirty years ago. People did not talk about divorce as a good experience through which they had passed and were helped to emerge as another self. But this is now becoming common conversation in the culture, for in our self-absorption, we generally think everything is all about us. Of course, this is something of a primal sin in the first place, but in our culture particularly, self-absorption takes the place of believing that we can actually make the world come to terms with us. If we do not understand that this is the cultural bent of our society, we will not understand how to preach the gospel to people who think all reality will come to terms with them rather than that the individual has to come to terms with reality.

Next is *self-transcendence*. This cultural motif explains why people today are so enamored of spirituality, and why they, if they can get away with it, will hear our preaching of the gospel as another spirituality. Walter Truett Anderson suggests that America in the twenty-first century has become the belief basket of the world. Most Americans think you can pick up bits and pieces from here and there—this spiritual practice, this idea, this thought, this theme, this name. The idea of self-transcendence suggests that this is exactly what our spiritual self is for. In other words, recognizing that there is a spiritual capacity within us, our culture suggests that it is nothing more than an extension of this project of the self.

Once again, if we do not think that the people who sit in our church pews are walking into church out of that world, we fool ourselves. Because of that, we must be extremely clear about even the most basic tenets of the Christian faith—the very *mono* in monotheism, for example. We are living in Canaan again, and Canaanite bookstores are all over the place, and our own people are reading Canaanite literature. This is once again a world of inherent polytheism, except that polytheism is now so morphed into a consumer reality that one buys this and buys that sometimes without even noticing it. All this is important only insofar as we understand that the people who walk into our churches and the people to whom we speak in our neighborhoods will not hear clearly what we say about the gospel unless we are at tremendous pains to make clear that we are not talking about self-transcendence. We are not talking about Christian discipleship as a project of the self.

I would also mention *self-enhancement*, the idea that we might even extend life. What other culture would have the kind of debate we have been having about whether baseball players should be able to take anabolic steroids and get away with it? We are living in a culture in which people are arguing about whether we ought to put an asterisk beside certain statistics in baseball. Not only so, but we are living in the midst of a culture in which that makes sense to people, and in which people think that they are not going to die, and in which people think that the project of the self can even extend to things like plastic surgery. We are living in a society in which it makes sense to some parents to give their daughters breast augmentation surgery as a high school graduation gift. What have we absorbed in the heart of this culture that would celebrate such a lie about what it means to be human? And lest we think it is just about someone else, we have to admit, this is very easy for all of us.

A final facet of our culture is *self-security*. We believe we are safe. We live in a world in which it makes sense not to worry. We have childproof caps on our medicine bottles. We have warnings on coffee cups from McDonald's that we ought not to drive with the beverage in our lap. We have vaccines, antibiotics, MRIs, and CAT scans. We have OSHA, and bumpers on our cars that are made to receive the impact and then return to normal. We are told to wear seat belts. We have a massive military and a police force. We have hospitals, and we think we are safe. We even extend this financially: we want to retire, we have investments, and we feel safe.

Most Christians throughout the history of Christianity, however, have not felt safe. Some time ago, I was reading a biography of Martin Luther, translated from the German, in which this biographer, who was not a believer, said that one has to understand that Luther was speaking to people who went to bed every night afraid they would die and go to hell before they woke up—thus the urgency of Luther's *anfechtungen*. He was afraid he would die and face a holy God before he would awaken again, because in the next room a monk could easily die thinking himself well when he went to bed. There were no antibiotics and no blood pressure tests, but famine, sword, pestilence, and plague were in ready supply. Christians shared with others the thought that this might be their last day, and thus there were things they had to keep in order. There were certain anxieties from which they could not escape. Obviously, this makes Luther difficult for us to understand, but more fundamentally and more importantly, it makes the gospel difficult for people to understand. People who are deeply convinced that they are safe will have a hard time understanding when a preacher tells them they are actually in perilous danger.

There is a sense, of course, in which the gospel is about safety.

In 1 Peter 1, for example, Peter writes to the church, and he begins with these words: "Peter, an apostle of Jesus Christ, To those who are elect exiles of the dispersion in Pontus, Galatia, Cappadocia, Asia, and Bithynia, according to the foreknowledge of God the Father, in the sanctification of the Spirit, for obedience to Jesus Christ and for sprinkling with his blood: May grace and peace be multiplied to you" (vv. 1–2). In chapter 2, he writes, "You are a chosen race, a royal priesthood, a holy nation, a people for his own possession, that you may proclaim the excellencies of him who called you out of darkness into his marvelous light. Once you were not a people, but now you are God's people; once you had not received mercy, but now you have received mercy" (vv. 9–10). *The English Standard Version* translates 1 Peter 1:1 with the phrase, "to those who are elect exiles." The *New American Standard Version*, on the other hand, translates that as "those who reside as aliens." I wonder if we really believe ourselves to be elect exiles of the dispersion.

Elect Exiles

Perhaps the most important thing to keep in mind as we consider the idea of preaching with the culture in view is that we are in fact elect exiles. We are here. We have an address in this world. We have a phone number. We wear certain clothes and speak a certain language, and we come out of a certain culture in which certain things make sense and other things do not make sense. But all of that is passing. It is all missiologically important, but it is eternally insignificant. We are elect exiles. The temptation for evangelicals in America is to believe something else, and to feel ourselves very much at home. I think that many of the tensions in evangelicalism today are the tensions felt by a people who are just beginning to awaken to the fact that this culture just might not be the friendly place we thought it to be. All of our cultural optimism is coming into question as we begin to look at the deeper levels of what is happening all around us, and we are beginning to realize that there is no ground for such optimism.

We cannot simply withdraw. That would be to deny our commission. But we cannot feel at home either. That would be to deny our identity. We are a chosen race, by God's grace, a royal priesthood, and so our task is to preach and teach the gospel in this City of Man until we see that eschatological vision of believers, the elect from every tongue and tribe and people and nation, standing before the throne of God. In that day, we will not be Americans, or Pontians, or Romans, or Cappadocians. We will be his.

CHAPTER 4

THE CENTER OF CHRISTIAN PREACHING: JUSTIFICATION BY FAITH

R. C. Sproul

Before expounding the essential points of the doctrine of justification—*sola fide*—I'd like to look at this doctrine's historical importance. Martin Luther stated that the doctrine of justification by faith alone is the article upon which the church stands or falls. I believe that it is the article upon which you and I stand or fall. John Calvin stated that *sola fide* is the hinge on which everything turns. The image of Atlas holding the weight of the world on his shoulders is one of the most descriptive metaphors for the doctrine. It was presented some years ago by J. I. Packer in his introduction to the English translation of Athanasius's *De incarnatione verbi Dei*. Dr. Packer said that *sola fide* is the Atlas upon which the whole of Christianity rests, so if Atlas were to shrug, the entire structure of the Christian faith would fall to the ground and shatter.

A Tempest in a Teapot?

But that's not the common assessment of the doctrine in our times. In the last few years I've heard *sola fide* described by many in the evangelical community—leaders, pastors, theologians—as the "small print" of the gospel. I've heard the Reformation debate reduced to nothing more than a large misunderstanding. One theologian calls the debate over *sola fide* a tempest in a teapot. A well-known and respected British theologian says that justification was a major issue in the sixteenth century, but that it is no longer a matter of serious debate. Most recently we've heard from a respected church historian that the Reformation is indeed over because, in the centuries since the Diet of Worms and the Council of Trent, Protestantism and Catholicism have mended their fences and now stand together. With the rise of the New Perspective on Paul, we have the further pronouncement of a pox on the houses of both Rome and the Reformers, because, they say, both sides completely misunderstood Paul's true teaching on justification. The real meaning has only recently been discovered by advocates of the New Perspective. We should not be surprised that this minimalist attitude is expressed widely in our day. It simply reflects the lessening significance of the doctrine of justification by faith alone.

Toward the end of his life, Martin Luther warned the church that in every generation the gospel will have to be reaffirmed because when the doctrine of justification by faith alone is boldly and accurately preached, it will produce conflict. Some of us must admit that we are among those who, when faced with the option of fight or flight, prefer to flee. We run away even though we are not threatened by burning at the stake; but many are, however, burned at the payroll of our local church if we insist on fidelity to the gospel.

The Roman Catholic View of Justification

Along with the lessening significance of *sola fide*, there is a widespread eclipse of the understanding of the doctrine. When I'm told that the Reformation is over, I can only guess that those who say this either don't understand Roman Catholic theology or Reformation theology. In fact, they probably don't understand both positions. For that reason I'd like to devote a few words to a brief reconnaissance over the historic Roman Catholic understanding of justification. In my years of seminary teaching, I've discovered that one of the best ways to help students grasp the distinctives of Reformation theology is to present them against the backdrop of Roman theology.

Let me begin this brief reconnaissance by stating that Rome did teach and continues to teach that justification is fundamentally a *sacerdotal* matter. Roman Catholics hold to the tradition that the grace of justification is administered by and through the church—by the priesthood through the sacraments. Specifically, Rome believes that justification begins with the sacrament of baptism, which is said to function by the automatic "working of the works" (*ex opere operato*). Although Rome doesn't like the word *automatic*, the concept is present in their belief system. In other words, the grace of justification is infused into the recipient of baptism, i.e., it is poured into their soul.

This grace of justification is sometimes defined as the righteousness of Christ that is poured into the soul; however, it does not justify the recipient *ex opere operato* because the receiver of the grace of baptism must cooperate with and assent to the work of grace. In Latin this is called *cooperare et assentire*, and the expression is used to indicate cooperation with and assent to that grace to such a degree that it leads to actual righteousness. Once you are righteous, you will be justified and remain in the state of grace as long as you keep yourself from mortal sin. In the Roman Catholic tradition, mortal sin, as distinguished from venial sin, kills the justifying grace that has been infused into the soul, so that a person who commits mortal sin loses his justifying grace.

On a parenthetical note, the Sixth Session of the Council of Trent makes it abundantly clear that authentic, genuine faith can and often does remain, even when mortal sin occurs and justifying grace is lost. So, according to Trent, a person can have real faith but lack justification. However, if mortal sin is committed and the grace of justification is thereby lost and demolished, the church has a remedy for that, the sacrament of penance, which the church defines as the second plank of justification for those who have made shipwreck of their souls. If someone loses justification through mortal sin, he won't get back his justification through another baptism because, even though losing the grace infused at baptism, he has not demolished the character *indelibus*—the indelible mark placed upon the soul at baptism. Instead, a second sacrament is needed and that sacrament is penance. This sacrament has several parts to it, including confession and priestly absolution.

Works of Satisfaction

Often Protestants misunderstand Roman Catholic confession. Protestants say: "I don't have to go to confession and confess my sins to a priest. Who does that priest think he is to say, 'I absolve you'? He doesn't have the authority to do that." But such thinking reflects an inaccurate understanding of Roman Catholic practice. Luther retained the confessional as do we. In most churches where corporate prayers of repentance are offered, the minister gives the people an assurance of pardon in the name of Christ. The Roman Catholic Church has never believed that the priest inherently, intrinsically, has the power to forgive. There is a tacit understanding that when the priest says "I absolve you," he does so as a representative of Jesus, who had said to his apostles, "Truly, I say to you, whatever you bind on earth shall be bound in heaven, and whatever you loose on earth shall be loosed in heaven" (Matt. 18:18).

The eye of the tornado in the sixteenth century was not confession given to the priest, but the final part of the sacrament of penance: the works of satisfaction. Such works achieve for the penitent sinner what the church defines as *congruous merit (meritum de congruo*), which is clearly distinguished from *condign merit* (*meritum de condigno*). Condign merit is merit that is so worthy and righteous that God would be unjust not to reward it; in other words, it is merit that requires or makes due a reward from God. However, condign merit is not as high as *supererogatory merit*, which only a few saints have been able to achieve.

Supererogatory merit is merit so manifold that it spills out and over, giving the believer more merit than he needs to enter heaven. The excess merit is then deposited in the treasury of merits and left at the church's disposal. The church has the power to transfer this excess merit and is free to draw from the treasury and apply it particularly to those in purgatory, who lack enough merit to make it into heaven. The abundant merit of Mary and of Joseph and of Saint Francis, for example, is deposited into the treasury of merit. This system was reaffirmed in the recently published Catholic catechism.

The congruous merit gained from the sacrament of penance is not considered on a par with either condign or supererogatory merit, but it is, nevertheless, real merit. In other words, if a believer does the works of satisfaction, such work makes it congruous, or fitting, for God to restore the believer once again to a state of grace and give him or her a new infusion of the righteousness needed. This view of righteousness lurked behind the indulgence controversy in the sixteenth century. For example, one way someone could supposedly gain works of satisfaction was by giving alms. Such giving was a work through which the penitent could be restored to a state of justification.

In terms of the doctrine of justification by faith alone, all too often Protestants slander the Roman Catholic Church by presenting a false division or separation between what we believe and what they believe. We Protestants often say: "We believe that justification is by faith; Rome believes it's by works. We believe justification comes by grace; Rome believes it's by merit. We believe

justification is by Christ; Rome believes it's through human effort."
That's slander because Rome has never taught those things. Rome
teaches that in order to be justified, a person must have faith.
During the sixteenth-century Council of Trent, in the Sixth Session,
before setting out the canons of anathema, the Council stated that
faith performs three functions in justification: the initiation (*ini-
tium*), foundation (*fundamentum*), and root (*radix*) of justification.
So the Council certainly maintained the importance of faith.

Necessary but Not Sufficient

So where does the Roman Catholic view differ from the Protestant
view? In the Roman Catholic view, faith is a necessary condition
for justification but not a sufficient condition. Fire and oxygen
illustrate the difference between a necessary condition and a sufficient condition. If we want to have a fire, we must have oxygen.
In most cases oxygen is a necessary condition for fire; without the
oxygen we cannot have a fire. But praise be to God that an oxygen supply is not a sufficient condition, because if it were, its very
presence would cause us to burst into flames. If oxygen were a
sufficient condition for fire, we'd burn with every breath.

The Protestant view, on the other hand, states that faith alone
is a sufficient condition. Where genuine faith exists, it links the
believer to Jesus and his righteousness, and it becomes the instrument
by which the believer is justified. That in itself is enough of a distinction to create a Reformation. The difference here is not between
faith and works but by faith and faith alone. Rome holds that "faith
plus works equals justification," whereas Protestants believe that
faith, if it is truly present, yields instant justification. The very fact
that Rome adheres to a sacrament of penance is a step away from
grace, since the sacrament requires a believer to do works of satisfaction to get that grace. In other words, grace must be merited. We
must acknowledge that grace is indeed a necessary tenet of Roman
Catholic doctrine; however, it is grace *plus* merit. Rome believes

that a person cannot be justified apart from Christ, but neither can anyone be justified apart from his or her own righteousness, which is carefully distinguished from the righteousness of Jesus.

Allow me to emphasize that the Roman Catholic doctrine of justification holds to the view that a believer does indeed need Christ to become righteous. However, the doctrine also holds that the righteousness that becomes the ground of someone's justification is not the righteousness by which Christ himself obeyed the things of God; it is instead a righteousness that inheres within the believer. Unless or until true righteousness inheres within someone, God will not declare that person just. Once again we see clearly that Rome teaches grace plus merit—Christ plus human righteousness—as the formula for redemption.

The Instrumental Cause of Justification

One of the great debates of the sixteenth century occurred over the instrumental cause of justification. A discussion about instrumental causality may seem a bit foreign to us, but throughout the ages, as early as Augustine, the church has used Aristotle's distinctions between different types of causes. Some of us learned in school about Aristotle's metaphor of the sculpture. Aristotle named several causes that work to turn a block of stone into a beautiful statue.

There is the *material cause*, the actual block of stone. The sculptor doesn't just call a statue into being; he must have a medium from which to make the statue. There must be a *formal cause*, a blueprint or a plan, before the sculptor can start. He doesn't just begin chipping away at the stone; he has an idea. Michelangelo used to say that he was not trying to create a statue, but, rather, to release the statue that he already envisioned to be imprisoned in the stone. Then there is the *final cause*, the purpose for which the statue is made. In centuries past, the final cause might have been a pope's request for a statue to beautify his garden or a mausoleum for his burial. However, the most important cause for

making a statue is the *efficient cause*, which is the sculptor himself. The efficient cause may be contrasted with the *instrumental
cause*—the tools, such as the chisel—that the sculptor uses to shape
the statue.

Applying Aristotle's distinctions to matters of justification, it's
clear that Rome holds to the belief that the instrumental cause,
the tool that brings about the desired result of justification, is first
the sacrament of baptism and second the sacrament of penance.
Although Roman Catholics recognize that the efficient cause of justification is the declaration of God, and that no one is justified until
or unless God declares him or her just, the instrumental cause of
justification in their view is baptism or penance.

The Reformers objected to Rome's view of justification, proclaiming that the instrumental cause is not found in the sacraments.
The only instrumental cause that links us to Christ and by which
God will declare us just is faith. Faith alone is the instrument of our
justification. This is of vital importance, because it points to the
truth that faith is not a work. Faith does not carry merit so that
those who have it hear God say: "You've done the right thing!
You're a good person; I will declare you righteous." No.

Defending the Doctrine

At this point Luther strongly emphasized that a justified person is,
at the same time, righteous and a sinner (*simul iustus et peccator*).
A Christian is *simul* (at the same time) *iustus* (just or righteous) and
peccator (a sinner). We get the words *impeccable* and *peccadillo*
from *peccare*. The idea that a justified person is simultaneously
righteous and a sinner gave the Catholic Church apoplexy. Rome
believed Luther's claim to be a monstrous lie. According to Rome,
God would never declare a person righteous if under scrutiny he
discovers that, in fact, they are not righteous. However, Luther said
this is exactly what God does. We see this in Genesis 15, where
Abraham believed God, and God reckoned him as righteous.

God reckons a sinner righteous by virtue of the single most important word in the whole debate: *imputation*. It is amazing how much of today's discussion and controversy focuses on this single idea of imputation. According to Luther, Calvin, and a magistrature of reformers, and according to the Bible, the only meritorious cause—the only ground—of justification is God's imputation of his righteousness to you, me, and all who believe.

John Piper is an example of one who upholds the doctrine of justification, and we owe him our gratitude for his labor of love on behalf of imputation and its central importance. Imputation is more than central; it's essential to the New Testament gospel. Friends, I beg you never to negotiate the concept of the imputed righteousness of Christ. That's the article upon which we stand and fall, because without his righteousness all we have to offer God is filthy rags. In the words of the psalmist, "If you, O LORD, should mark iniquities, O Lord, who could stand?" (Ps. 130:3). Our only hope in life and death is the righteousness of Christ. This is no abstract theological doctrine; this is all of it.

As John Piper declares, it's important for us not just to believe the doctrine of justification by faith alone, but also to defend this doctrine. He adds that it's not enough to believe and defend it: we must contend for it with our all.

> *Let goods and kindred go, this mortal life also;*
> *The body they may kill: God's truth abideth still,*
> *His kingdom is forever.*

The righteousness by which we are justified is an alien righteousness (*ustitium alienum*), a foreign righteousness. If this expression is unclear to you, know that Luther also described justification as a righteousness that is outside of us (*extra nos*), apart from us. The only righteousness that will justify us is the righteousness of Christ. We are naked and helpless without the cloak of his righteousness covering us. We are foul in God's sight until he imputes to us the righteousness of Christ.

Not Profession but Possession

We are not justified by the doctrine of justification by faith. We can believe this doctrine, give intellectual assent to its truth, and even contend for it with our all without ever having the faith that alone will justify us. Our justification is not accomplished by a profession of faith. The evangelical world has never fully grasped that nobody is justified by a simple profession of faith. Professions of faith are good things, and those who believe are supposed to profess what they believe, but it's the "possession" of faith—not its "profession"—that translates a person from the kingdom of darkness into the kingdom of light.

For that reason we who are preachers must be very careful how we preach the gospel, to guard against giving people a false sense of security, saying, "If you raise your hand . . . if you come to the altar . . . if you sign the card . . . you're going to get into the kingdom of God." We wind up constructing all kinds of distorted theology to account for false professions of faith. We must remember that it is not the doctrine that saves anybody; the doctrine simply describes what brings us into a state of justification.

When I became a Christian on September 13, 1957, at 11:00 p.m., I had never heard the word *justification*. I didn't know what it was. I had never read the Bible, although I'd heard about Jesus. The night I became a Christian, a man sat me down and told me about Christ. He quoted from the book of Ecclesiastes:

> *If the clouds are full of rain,*
> *they empty themselves on the earth,*
> *and if a tree falls to the south or to the north,*
> *in the place where the tree falls, there it will lie. (Eccl. 11:3)*

That Scripture verse was illuminated by the Holy Ghost, and I saw myself as that fallen tree in the middle of the forest, lying there and rotting away. I am perhaps the only person in the history of the church who has been converted by that verse. That night I went back to my room overwhelmed by a sense of my sin and by the conviction that my only hope in life and death was the atoning work of my Savior. Beside my bed I fell on my knees. I didn't recite the catechism; I simply said, "O God, forgive me for my sins." I arose justified.

The first time I read the New Testament, I read the story Jesus told about the Pharisee and the tax collector. The Pharisee prayed, "God, I thank you that I am not like other men, extortioners, unjust, adulterers, or even like this tax collector. I fast twice a week; I give tithes of all that I get" (Luke 18:11–12). The tax collector, on the other hand, couldn't even lift his eyes to heaven. All he could do was cry out, "God, be merciful to me, a sinner!" (18:13). Most of Jesus' parables are difficult to understand, but this one ends clearly. Jesus concluded, "I tell you, this man went down to his house justified, rather than the other. For everyone who exalts himself will be humbled, but the one who humbles himself will be exalted" (v. 14). Which of the two men went to his home justified? The one who, by faith, was covered by the righteousness of Christ.

No Other Gospel!

The gospel is good news. For that reason, and because I love my Catholic friends, I weep for their gospel which is no gospel. It's a bad gospel. It's bad news. As Paul said to the Galatians, "Even if we or an angel from heaven should preach to you a gospel contrary to the one we preached to you, let him be accursed" (Gal. 1:8). The Greek word Paul used so forcefully here is *anathema*, "let him be anathema." Paul is emphatic that even if an angel comes preaching a different gospel, the angel must be taken by the seat of his ethereal pants and thrown out the door.

Paul writes such strong words because there is no other gospel. He adds: "As we have said before, so now I say again: If anyone is preaching to you a gospel contrary to the one you received, let him be accursed. . . . For am I now seeking the approval of man, or of God? Or am I trying to please man? If I were still trying to please man, I would not be a servant of Christ" (vv. 9–10).

To summarize, the Roman view of justification starts with baptism. The benefits that accrue from baptism can be lost by committing mortal sin, but they can be recovered by penance. The regained justification lasts until another mortal sin is committed, and the cycle repeats. According to the Roman view, a believer's destiny is determined by the purity of his heart at the time of death. Even if the believer does not die in a state of impenitent mortal sin, there may be impurities on the soul, necessitating purgatory until the impurities are cleansed.

All of this is presented in the most recent Roman Catholic catechism. It states that if a believer has any impurities on his or her soul at the time of death, the believer will go to purgatory. The soul of the believer may be in purgatory for only a week if he or she is near to sainthood, but more likely the believer will remain there for several hundred years—perhaps even two million, three million, or four million years—until, in that place of purging, the believer is so cleansed from impurities that finally, when God looks at him or her, he sees an inherent righteousness.

Is that good news? It is actually the worst possible news we can hear. If someone told me that the only way I could get into the kingdom of heaven and be adopted into the family of God is to get rid of all impurities in my soul, I would despair. So let me tell you what the good news is. I despair of my righteousness; I acknowledge my sin. I put my trust in Christ and Christ alone. And the good news is that at the very instant I do, all that Jesus is, and all that

Jesus has, is mine, and for the rest of my days he has me covered. The Father looks beyond my impurities and all my sin, and he sees the cloak of the righteousness of Jesus. For that reason, I am justified not for today, not for this week, not until I commit another sin, but for eternity. Is there any better news than that in the whole world?

Beloved, explaining the doctrine of justification by faith alone is really a simple matter. The doctrine is not difficult. In fact, the doctrine was always easy to teach to my seminary students. They understood it. Still, I warned them to be careful, because although they may grasp it in the head, it's another matter completely to grasp it in the bloodstream. That is why we must have the doctrine of justification by faith alone preached over and over and over. At the front door of the church the enemy lies in wait to whisper in our ears as we walk across that threshold: "You have to make sure. Your merits count. Righteousness has got to be inherent, so you are going to lose your justification the next time you break the law." When I hear that, I rebuke him with the words of the apostle Paul: "Who shall bring any charge against God's elect? It is God who justifies. Who is to condemn? Christ Jesus is the one who died—more than that, who was raised—who is at the right hand of God, who indeed is interceding for us" (Rom. 8:33–34). It is God who justifies. It is God who redeems the ungodly. Don't move from that truth, no matter what comes.

CHAPTER 5

PREACHING AS EXPOSITORY EXULTATION FOR THE GLORY OF GOD

John Piper

In this chapter I will first reflect on the kind of preaching that I long to see God raise up in our day—the kind that is shaped by the weight of the glory of God. Second, I will try to portray the glory of God, which affects preaching this way. Third, I will offer my biblical understanding of how people awaken to this glory and are changed by it. Finally, I will explain how all of this calls for a kind of preaching that I call *expository exultation*.

Reflections on the Kind of Preaching Produced by the Weight of God's Glory

George Whitefield believed in preaching and gave his life to it, and by his preaching God did a mighty work of salvation on both sides of the Atlantic. Whitefield's biographer, Arnold Dallimore, chronicles the astonishing effect that Whitefield's preaching had in Britain and America in the eighteenth century. It came like rain on the parched land and made the desert spring forth with the flowers of righteousness. Dallimore lifts his eyes from the transformed wasteland of Whitefield's time and expresses his longing that God would do this again. He cries out for a new generation of preachers like Whitefield. His words help me express what I long for in the coming generations of preachers in America and around the world. Dallimore says:

> Yea . . . that we shall see the great Head of the Church once more . . . raise up unto Himself certain young men whom He may use in this glorious employ. And what manner of men will they be? Men mighty in the Scriptures, their lives dominated by a sense of the greatness, the majesty and holiness of God, and their minds and hearts aglow with the great truths of the doctrines of grace. They will be men who have learned what it is to die to self, to human aims and personal ambitions; men who are willing to be "fools for Christ's sake", who will bear reproach and falsehood, who will labor and suffer, and whose supreme desire will be, not to gain earth's accolades, but to win the Master's approbation when they appear before His awesome judgment seat. They will be men who will preach with broken hearts and tear-filled eyes, and upon whose ministries God will grant an extraordinary effusion of the Holy Spirit, and who will witness "signs and wonders following" in the transformation of multitudes of human lives.[1]

Mighty in the Scriptures, aglow with the great truths of the doctrines of grace, dead to self, willing to labor and suffer, indifferent to the accolades of man, broken for sin, *and dominated by a sense of the greatness, and majesty, and holiness of God—* Dallimore, like Whitefield, believed that preaching is the heralding of God's word from that kind of heart. Preaching is not conversation. Preaching is not discussion. Preaching is not casual talk about religious things. Preaching is not simply teaching. Preaching is the heralding of a message permeated by the sense of

---

[1] Arnold Dallimore, *George Whitefield* (Edinburgh: Banner of Truth, 1970), 1:16.

God's greatness and majesty and holiness. The topic may be anything under the sun, but it is always brought into the blazing light of God's greatness and majesty in his word. That was the way Whitefield preached.

In the last century no one embodied that view better than Martyn Lloyd-Jones, who served the Westminster Chapel in London for thirty years. When J. I. Packer was a twenty-two-year-old student, he heard Lloyd-Jones preach every Sunday evening in London during the school year of 1948–1949. He said that he had "never heard such preaching." (That's why so many people say so many minimizing and foolish things about preaching—they have never heard true preaching; they have no basis for judgment about the usefulness of true preaching.) Packer said it came to him "with the force of electric shock, bringing . . . more of a sense of God than any other man" he had known.[2] That's what Dallimore meant. Oh, that God would raise up young preachers who leave their hearers with a spiritual sense of shock at the sense of God—some sense of the infinite weight of the reality of God.

That is my longing for our day—and for you. That God would raise up thousands of broken-hearted, Bible-saturated preachers who are dominated by a sense of the greatness and the majesty and the holiness of God, revealed in the gospel of Christ crucified and risen, and reigning with absolute authority over every nation and every army and every false religion and every terrorist and every tsunami and every cancer cell and every galaxy in the universe.

God did not ordain the cross of Christ or create the lake of fire[3] in order to communicate the insignificance of belittling his glory. The death of the Son of God and the damnation of unrepentant human beings are the loudest shouts under heaven that

---

[2] Christopher Catherwood, *Five Evangelical Leaders* (Wheaton, IL: Harold Shaw, 1985), 170.
[3] Jesus said in Luke 22:22 that the cross was "determined [ὡρισμενον] by God," and in Matthew 25:41 that the fires of hell were prepared by God. "Then he will say to those on his left, 'Depart from me, you cursed, into the eternal fire prepared for the devil and his angels.'"

God is infinitely holy, and sin is infinitely offensive, and wrath is infinitely just, and grace is infinitely precious, and our brief life—and the life of every person in your church and in your community—leads to everlasting joy or everlasting suffering. If our preaching does not carry the weight of these things to our people, what will? *Veggie Tales?* Radio? Television? Discussion groups? Emergent conversations?

God planned for his Son to be crucified (Rev. 13:8; 2 Tim. 1:9) and for hell to be terrible (Matt. 25:41) so that we would have the clearest witnesses possible to what is at stake when we preach. What gives preaching its seriousness is that the mantle of the preacher is soaked with the blood of Jesus and singed with the fire of hell. That's the mantle that turns mere talkers into preachers. Yet tragically some of the most prominent evangelical voices today diminish the horror of the cross and the horror of hell—the one stripped of its power to bear our punishment, and the other demythologized into self-dehumanization and the social miseries of this world.[4]

Oh, that the rising generations would see that the world is

---

[4] From the American scene consider this breathtaking comment by Joel Green that flies in the face of what the church has believed is central to the gospel and what is grounded in clear Scriptures (Isa. 53:4–6, 8–10; Gal. 3:13; Rom. 8:3): "Whatever meaning the atonement had, it would be a grave error to imagine that it focused on assuaging God's anger or winning God's merciful attention. . . . [T]he Scriptures as a whole provide no ground for a portrait of an angry God needing to be appeased in atoning sacrifice. . . . Whatever else can be said of Paul's understanding of the death of Jesus, his theology of the cross lacks any developed sense of divine retribution." Joel Green and Mark Baker, *Recovering the Scandal of the Cross: Atonement in New Testament & Contemporary Context* (Downers Grove, IL: InterVarsity, 2000), 51, 56. From the British scene Steve Chalke calls the teaching that Christ bore the wrath of God in our place "cosmic child abuse": "The fact is that the cross isn't a form of cosmic child abuse—a vengeful Father, punishing his Son for an offense he has not even committed. Understandably, both people inside and outside of the Church have found this twisted version of events morally dubious and a huge barrier to faith. Deeper than that, however, is that such a concept stands in total contradiction to the statement 'God is love'. If the cross is a personal act of violence perpetrated by God towards humankind but borne by his Son, then it makes a mockery of Jesus' own teaching to love your enemies and to refuse to repay evil with evil." *The Lost Message of Jesus* (Grand Rapids, MI: Zondervan, 2004), 182–83. N. T. Wright argues that "most" (does he mean "all"?) of the references to hell in the New Testament are not talking about a place of eternal conscious suffering, but that we need a "reconstruction" or "restatement" of the doctrine of hell "in the present day" (1) in terms of humans using their "gift of freedom" to "dehumanize themselves completely," and (2) in terms of social injustice and misery: "There is an equally proper and yet more necessary biblical doctrine of hell in terms of human social and corporate life on this earth." *Following Jesus: Biblical Reflections on Discipleship* (Grand Rapids, MI: Eerdmans, 1994), 95–96.

not overrun with a sense of seriousness about God. There is no surplus in the church of a sense of God's glory; there is no excess of earnestness in the church about heaven and hell and sin and salvation, and, therefore, the joy of many Christians is paper thin. By the millions, people are amusing themselves to death with DVDs and 107-inch TV screens and games on their cell phones, and slapstick worship while the spokesmen of a massive world religion write letters to the West in major publications: "The first thing we are calling you to is Islam. . . . It is the religion of enjoining the good and forbidding the evil with the hand, tongue and heart. It is the religion of jihad in the way of Allah so that Allah's Word and religion reign Supreme."[5] And then these spokesmen publicly bless suicide bombers who blow up children in front of falafel shops and call it the way to paradise. This is the world in which we preach.

And yet incomprehensibly, in this Christ-diminishing, soul-destroying age, books and seminars and divinity schools and church growth specialists are bent on saying to young pastors, "lighten up," "get funny," and "do something amusing." To this I ask, Where is the spirit of Jesus? "If anyone would come after me, let him deny himself and take up his cross and follow me. For whoever would save his life will lose it, but whoever loses his life for my sake will find it" (Matt. 16:24–25). "If your right eye causes you to sin, tear it out and throw it away. For it is better that you lose one of your members than that your whole body be thrown into hell" (Matt. 5:29). "Any one of you who does not renounce all that he has cannot be my disciple" (Luke 14:33). "If anyone comes to me and does not hate his own father and mother and wife and children and brothers and sisters, yes, and even his own life, he cannot be my disciple" (Luke 14:26). "Follow me,

<hr>

[5] Quoted from "The Islam/West Debate: Documents from a Global Debate on Terrorism, U. S. Policy and the Middle East," ed. David Blankenhorn in *First Things*, March 2006, 161: 71.

and leave the dead to bury their own dead" (Matt. 8:22). "Whoever would be first among you must be slave of all" (Mark 10:44). "Fear him who can destroy both soul and body in hell" (Matt. 10:28). "Some of you they will put to death. . . . But not a hair of your head will perish. By your endurance you will gain your lives" (Luke 21:16-19).

Would the church growth counsel to Jesus be, "Lighten up, Jesus. Do something amusing," and to the young pastor, "Whatever you do, young pastor, don't be like the Jesus of the Gospels. Lighten up"? From my perspective, which feels very close to eternity these days, that message to pastors sounds increasingly insane.

A Portrayal of the Glory of God

What you believe about the necessity of preaching and the nature of preaching is governed by your sense of the greatness and the glory of God and how you believe people awaken to that glory and live for that glory. So this next section presents a portrayal of the glory of God, and the third will deal with how people awaken to that glory and are changed by it.

From beginning to end, nothing in the Bible is more ultimate in the mind and heart of God than the glory of God—the beauty of God, the radiance of his manifold perfections. At every point in God's revealed action, wherever he makes plain the ultimate goal of that action, the goal is always the same: to uphold and display his glory.

- He predestined us for his glory (Eph. 1:5–6).
- He created us for his glory (Isa. 43:7).
- He elected Israel for his glory (Jer. 13:11).
- He saved his people from Egypt for his glory (Ps. 106:8).
- He rescued them from exile for his glory (Isa. 48:9–11).

- He sent Christ into the world so that Gentiles would praise God for his glory (Rom. 15:9).
- He commands his people, whether they eat or drink, to do all things for his glory (1 Cor. 10:31).
- He will send Jesus a second time so that all the redeemed will marvel at his glory (2 Thess. 1:9–10).
- Therefore, the mission of the church is: "Declare his glory among the nations, his marvelous works among all the peoples" (Ps. 96:3).

These and a hundred more places drive us back up into the ultimate allegiance of God. Nothing affects preaching more deeply than to be struck almost speechless—almost—by the passion of God for the glory of God. What is clear from the whole range of biblical revelation is that God's ultimate allegiance is to know himself perfectly, and to love himself infinitely, and to share this experience, as much as it can be, with his people. Over every act of God flies the banner: "For my own sake, for my own sake, I do it, for how should my name be profaned? My glory I will not give to another" (Isa. 48:11; cf. 42:8).

From all eternity the ever-existing, never-becoming, always-perfect God has known himself and loved what he knows. He has eternally seen his beauty and savored what he sees. His understanding of his own reality is flawless, and his exuberance in enjoying it is infinite. He has no needs, for he has no imperfections. He has no inclinations to evil because he has no deficiencies that could tempt him to do wrong. He is therefore the holiest and happiest being that is or that can be conceived. We cannot conceive of a happiness greater than the happiness of infinite power delighting infinitely in infinite beauty in the personal fellowship of the Trinity.

To share this experience—the experience of knowing and enjoying his glory—is the reason God created the world. He would bring us to know him and to enjoy him the way he knows himself and the way he enjoys himself. Indeed, his purpose is that the very knowledge that he has of himself and the very joy that he has in himself will be our knowledge and our enjoyment, so that we know him with his own knowledge and we enjoy him with his own joy. This is the ultimate meaning of Jesus' prayer in John 17:26 where he asks his Father "that the love with which you have loved me may be in them, and I in them." The Father's knowledge of and joy in "the radiance of the glory of God" (Heb. 1:3)—whose name is Jesus Christ—will be in us because Jesus is in us.

And if you ask: How does God's aim to share this experience (of knowing himself and enjoying himself) relate to the love of God? the answer is: his aim to share that experience *is* the love of God. God's love is his commitment to share the knowledge and enjoyment of his glory with us. When John says that God is love (1 John 4:8, 16), he means that it is God's nature to share the enjoyment of his glory, even if it costs him the life of his Son.

This means that God's aim to display his glory and our delight in that glory are in perfect harmony. We do not honor fully what we don't enjoy. God is not glorified fully in merely being known; he is glorified by being known and enjoyed so deeply that our lives become a display of his worth.

Jesus said two things to emphasize his role in giving us the knowledge and the joy of God. He said, "No one *knows* the Father except the Son and anyone to whom the Son chooses to reveal him" (Matt. 11:27). And he said, "These things I have spoken to you, that *my joy* may be in you, and that your joy may be full" (John 15:11). In other words, we know the Father *with the knowledge of the Son*, and we enjoy the Father *with the joy of the Son*. Jesus has made us partakers of his own knowledge of God and his own enjoyment of God.

The way this becomes visible in the world is not mainly by

passionate acts of corporate worship on Sunday morning—as precious as those moments are—but by the changes that it produces in our lives. Jesus said, "Let your light shine before others, so that they may see your good works and give glory to your Father who is in heaven" (Matt. 5:16). The light that shines through our deeds and causes people to see God is the all-satisfying worth of his glory.

It works something like this: When the glory of God is the treasure of our lives, we will not lay up treasures on earth, but spend them for the spread of his glory. We will not covet, but overflow with liberality. We will not crave the praise of men, but forget ourselves in praising God. We will not be mastered by sinful, sensual pleasures, but sever their root by the power of a superior promise. We will not nurse a wounded ego or cherish a grudge or nurture a vengeful spirit, but will hand over our cause to God and bless those who hate us. *Every sin flows from the failure to treasure the glory of God above all things.* Therefore one crucial, visible way to display the truth and value of the glory of God is by humble, sacrificial lives of service that flow only from the fountain of God's all satisfying glory.

How People Waken to This Glory and Are Changed by It

We turn now to the question of how people are wakened to the glory of God and are changed by it. One essential part of the answer is given by the apostle Paul in 2 Corinthians 3:18–4:6. He writes, "And we all, with unveiled face, beholding the glory of the Lord, are being transformed into the same image from one degree of glory to another. For this comes from the Lord who is the Spirit" (v. 18). Beholding the glory of the Lord, we are transformed from one degree of glory to another. This is God's way of changing people into the image of his Son so that they reflect the glory of the

Lord. To be changed in the way that glorifies God, we fix our gaze on the glory of the Lord.[6]

How does this happen? (And here we are moving very close to the implications for preaching.) Paul explains in 2 Corinthians 4:3-4 how we behold the glory of the Lord.

> Even if our gospel is veiled, it is veiled only to those who are perishing. In their case the god of this world has blinded the minds of the unbelievers, to keep them from seeing [here is the fulfillment of 2 Cor. 3:18] the light of the gospel of the glory of Christ, who is the image of God.

We behold the glory of the Lord most clearly and most crucially in the gospel, so much so that Paul calls it "the gospel of the glory of Christ," which means—and this has enormous implications for preaching—that in this dispensation, when we cannot see the glory of the Lord directly as we will when he returns in the clouds, we see it most clearly by means of *his Word*. The gospel is a *message* in words. Paradoxically, words are *heard* and glory is *seen*. Therefore, Paul is saying that we see the glory of Christ not mainly with our eyes but through our *ears*. "Faith comes from hearing, and hearing through the word of Christ" (Rom. 10:17) because seeing the glory of Christ comes through hearing, and hearing through the gospel of Christ.

Consider how this was expressed in the life of the prophet Samuel. In the days of Samuel, there was no frequent vision of the Lord (1 Sam. 3:1)—just like today where there is a famine of seeing and savoring the glory of God. But then God raised up a new

---

[6] Beware of saying, "It doesn't work," and then turning to other techniques and leaving behind God's way of changing people. You may be able to change people with ways and means different from this process of seeing the glory of the Lord in the Word of God, but will it be a change that magnifies the glory of Christ? Not all change honors Christ. Paul sounds this warning with the words at the beginning of 2 Cor. 4:3, "And even if our gospel is veiled, it is veiled only to those who are perishing." In other words, he admits that his gospel does not change everyone. The "perishing" do not see the glory of God in the gospel. Paul does not change his strategy because of this. Neither should we.

prophet, and how did God appear to him? The same way he will appear to you and your people. First Samuel 3:21, "And the LORD appeared again at Shiloh, for the LORD revealed *himself* to Samuel at Shiloh *by the word of the LORD*." He revealed *himself* by the *word*. This is how our people will behold the glory of the Lord, and be changed into the kind of people who make his glory known. Paul tells us now that the word that reveals the glory of God most clearly and centrally is the gospel (2 Cor. 4:4).

The Implicit Call for Expository Exultation

This brings me finally to a concluding point on preaching as *expository exultation*. If it is the purpose of God that we display his glory in the world, and if we display it because we have been changed by knowing and enjoying it, and if we know and enjoy it by beholding the glory of the Lord, and if we behold that glory most clearly and centrally in the gospel of the glory of Christ, and if the gospel is a message delivered in words to the world, then what follows is that God intends for preachers to unfold these words and exult over them—which is what I call expository *exultation*.

Each word matters. It is *expository* because there is so much about the gospel that cries out to be exposited (opened, unfolded, elucidated, clarified, explained, displayed). We see this when we focus on five essential dimensions of the gospel message:

1) The gospel is a message about *historical events*—the life and death and resurrection of Christ—summoning us to open them with thorough expositions of texts.
2) The gospel is a message about what those events *achieved* before we experienced anything or even existed—the completion of perfect obedience, the payment for our sins, the removal of the wrath of God, the installation of Jesus as the crucified and risen Messiah and king of the universe, the disarming of the rulers and authorities, the destruction of

death—all of these summoning us to open them with thorough expositions of texts.

3) The gospel is a message about the *transfer* of these achievements from Christ to particular persons through our union with Christ by faith alone apart from works, which summons us to open for our people the nature and dynamics of faith by the exposition of dozens of texts.

4) The gospel is a message about the *good things that are now true about us* as the achievement of the cross is applied to us in Christ—that God is only merciful to us now instead of wrathful (propitiation); that we are counted righteous in Christ now (justification); that we are freed now from the guilt and power of sin (redemption); that we are positionally and progressively made holy (sanctification)—all of which summons us to open these glorious realities for our people week after week with thorough expositions of texts.

5) Finally the gospel is a message about the glorious *God himself* as our final, eternal, all-satisfying Treasure. "We . . . rejoice *in God* through our Lord Jesus Christ, through whom we have now received reconciliation" (Rom. 5:11). The gospel we preach is "the gospel *of the glory of Christ who is the image of God* (2 Cor. 4:4)." If our gospel stops short of this goal—enjoying God himself, not just his gifts of forgiveness and rescue from hell and eternal life—then we are not preaching the gospel of the glory of God in the face of Christ (2 Cor. 4:6). Our ultimate goal is knowing and enjoying God. As we saw in the beginning of this chapter, that is why we were created—that God might share with us the knowledge and enjoyment of himself. This is what it means for him to love us. This is what the cross ultimately obtained for us. And this too, by every text of Scripture—all of it inspired by God to awaken hope in his glory (2 Tim. 3:16–17; Rom. 15:4)—calls for the richest exposition that our people may be fed the best and highest food of heaven.

Exposition of texts is essential because the gospel is a message that comes to us in words, and God has ordained that people see the glory of Christ—the "unsearchable riches of Christ" (Eph. 3:8)—in those gospel words. That is our calling: to open the words and sentences and paragraphs of Scripture and display "the glory of Christ who is the image of God."

This leads us finally to the second word in the phrase *expository exultation*. Woe to us if we do our exposition of such a gospel without *exultation*—that is, without exulting over the truth we unfold. When Paul writes, "For what we *proclaim* is not ourselves, but Jesus Christ as Lord" (2 Cor. 4:5), the word he uses for *proclaim* is κηρύσσομεν —we *herald* Christ as Lord, we *announce* Christ as Lord. The κῆρυξ —the proclaimer, the "preacher" (1 Tim. 2:7; 2 Tim. 1:11)—may have to explain what he is saying if people don't understand (so teaching may be involved). But what sets the herald apart from the philosopher, and scribe, and teacher is that he is the herald of news—and in our case, infinitely good news, infinitely valuable news, the greatest news in all the world.

The Creator of the universe, who is more glorious and more to be desired than any treasure on earth, has revealed himself in Jesus Christ to be known and enjoyed forever by anyone in the world who will lay down the arms of rebellion, receive his blood-bought amnesty, and embrace his Son as Savior, Lord, and Treasure of their lives.

Oh, brothers, do not lie about the value of the gospel by the dullness of your demeanor. Exposition of the most glorious reality is a glorious reality. If it is not expository *exultation*—authentic, from the heart—something false is being said about the value of the gospel. Don't say by your face, or by your voice, or by your life that the gospel is not the gospel of the all-satisfying glory of Christ. It is. And may God raise up from among you a generation of preachers whose exposition is worthy of the truth of God and whose exultation is worthy of the glory of God.

CHAPTER 6

THE PASTOR'S PRIORITIES: WATCH YOUR LIFE AND DOCTRINE

C. J. Mahaney

"Keep a close watch on yourself and on the teaching. Persist in this, for by so doing you will save both yourself and your hearers" (1 Tim. 4:16). If my historical hero, Charles Spurgeon, had been asked to contribute to a volume such as this one, I suspect he may have opened with these penetrating words from the apostle Paul. I have good reason for such speculation, for in his classic *Lectures to My Students*—a collection of addresses delivered at his much beloved Pastors College—1 Timothy 4:16 serves as an epigraph to the opening chapter, "The Minister's Self-Watch."

This prince of preachers knew from experience that a steady grip on these two sentences would protect, guide, and reassure young men in the ministry. Yet, his weighty charge merely echoed the words of the original pastor of pastors—the author of 1 Timothy, the apostle Paul. Writing as a father to his dear and true son in the faith, Paul is intimately acquainted with Timothy's frailties and the perils of pastoral ministry in a sinful world. He opens his letter by laying a foundation of imperative doctrinal issues and critical leadership responsibilities. But then Paul gets personal, and not just personal with Timothy; he gets personal with you and me, for we were all in Paul's peripheral vision as he penned these words—you and I and every man who would ever be called by God into Christian ministry.

More importantly, the sovereign God who inspired this passage had us in view. God, who saved us and called us into ministry, wants to have a word with us, a very personal word. The Savior wants to silence the shouts of professional demands and care for you personally with these words: "Keep a close watch on yourself and on the teaching. Persist in this . . ." In its essence, this is our job description as pastors; and it is followed closely by the fruit of faithful ministry.

" . . . for by so doing you will save both yourself and your hearers." Do you feel the weight of this verse upon your soul? The stakes could not be higher. Nothing less than the preservation of yourself and your congregation hang upon the God-appointed means of your faithful pastoral ministry. The implications couldn't be more serious. They are, in fact, eternal.

Our Twofold Task

Watch yourself and watch your teaching. Or, as the NIV renders this verse, "Watch your life and doctrine closely." First Timothy 4:16 requires us to pay *equally* close attention to *both*. While it is appropriate, even necessary, to distinguish between life and doctrine, the two are ultimately inseparable. I cannot watch my life accurately unless I understand sound doctrine, and it does me no good whatsoever to study doctrine unless I also apply it to my life. Thus, we must not watch one to the neglect of the other; we must give full and uncompromised attention to both. And we must watch closely and consistently, not casually or occasionally.

Then there is the matter of that little pronoun *yourself*. Paul's words to Timothy are an expression of God's perfect wisdom for our good, and it begins, "Keep a close watch on *yourself* . . ." But often we behave as if this verse were directed at someone, anyone, *other than* ourselves. We watch over the souls entrusted to our care and yet neglect our own soul. We pay close, even diligent, attention to the life and doctrine of our church members, all the while ignoring the inner workings of our own heart. While caring for the flock is certainly our pastoral responsibility, the command in this verse is unequivocal. Watch *your* life. Watch *your* doctrine. Watch them equally and watch them closely.

Watch Your Life

Ah, but one task is easier than the other, is it not? Don't you find it far more appealing and enjoyable to study doctrine than to study your heart? Isn't it much more pleasant to examine your books than to examine your motives? Aren't we far quicker to apply ourselves to a specific text in preparation for a sermon than to apply that same text to our heart and life? Puritan Richard Baxter wrote: "It is a palpable error of some ministers . . . who study hard to preach exactly, yet study little or not at all to live exactly."[1]

Sound Doctrine Is Not Enough

Not long ago I was privileged to attend John MacArthur's annual Shepherd's Conference for pastors. At the conclusion of one of the sessions, I exited the sanctuary and immediately became aware of a charged atmosphere in the outdoor lobby. Men all around me had quickened their pace. Their faces were uniformly alert and all eyes were fixed in the same direction. In a moment I identified the source of their excitement: free books. We all know that few things thrill the heart of a pastor more than books. Free books send us into a frenzy. I love what this episode says about pastors

---

[1] Richard Baxter, *The Reformed Pastor* (Carlisle, PA: Banner of Truth, 1974), 63–64.

in general and those pastors in particular: the pastors I know well place a high value on any resource that can provide insight into the Word of God. They understand that a knowledge of Scripture is essential to their ministry.

However, we can often forget that a knowledge of Scripture alone is not sufficient. Of course, James won't let us forget that we must "Be doers of the word, and not hearers only, deceiving yourselves" (James 1:22). This verse tells us that apart from obedience, knowledge can be deceptive. This puts an interesting twist on some of the favorite activities of good evangelical pastors: attending ministerial conferences, listening to sermons, and reading doctrinally sound books. All such activities afford us the opportunity for serious progress in personal godliness and ministry effectiveness. Yet each one can also be an instrument of progressive self-deception.

The problem occurs when we assume that merely attending a conference, or listening to a sermon, or reading a book signifies actual change. (I understand the power of this deception. I can often feel like I'm maturing spiritually simply by *obtaining* new books!) We can even be deeply moved by profound scriptural truth but never actually grow in godliness. In his commentary on the epistle of James, Peter Davids elaborates, "No matter how extensive one's scriptural knowledge, how amazing one's memory, it is self-deception if that is all there is. True knowledge is the prelude to action, and it is obedience to the Word that counts in the end."[2]

As pastors, our lives can be filled with reading, studying, sermon preparation, sermon proclamation, and counseling. Ironically, a busy schedule of absorbing and communicating truth can leave little time for *practicing* truth. But truth must be proclaimed and *then* applied, heard and *then* obeyed, preached and *then* prac-

---

[2] Peter H. Davids, *New International Biblical Commentary: James* (Peabody, MA: Hendrickson, 1983), 41.

ticed, for until I *practice* truth, I will not experience the transforming effect of truth on my soul. Faith practices truth by crying
out to God in the midst of suffering. Love practices truth by actions
of kindness and patience. Humility practices truth by specific confession of sin. Forgiveness practices truth by overlooking an
offense. Hope practices truth by recalling the mercies of God.
Indeed, I have never truly, fully learned truth until I have *prac-
ticed* truth.

In this book, you will encounter much rich truth. I hope you read
every chapter, and more than once if necessary. But please understand: according to James, if you consume truth without applying
truth, you risk the false and dangerous impression that spiritual
growth was achieved without application. But it never is—never.
We must be ever wary of the self-deception of which James speaks.
Let's recognize the limitations of sound doctrine, and make the
practice of truth a daily priority. Never stop watching your life.

The Consequences of Neglect

Sound doctrine is not enough, because, according to Scripture,
the fundamental qualification for pastoral ministry is godly character. Neither skill, nor knowledge, nor wisdom, nor reputation,
nor personality, nor apparent fruitfulness of public ministry will
suffice. Scan 1 Timothy 3 and Titus 1, and you will encounter a
profile of personal piety.

Yes, the pastor must be able to teach. Certainly, he must handle the Word of truth accurately and skillfully. But the foundational
assumption of Scripture—both for appointment to or continuation
in ministry—is that the pastor provides a godly example, not a *perfect* example but an authentic one. As Spurgeon exhorted his students, "Our characters must be more persuasive than our speech."[3]

---

[3] C. H. Spurgeon, "The Minister's Self-Watch," in *Lectures to My Students* (Pasadena, TX:
Pilgrim Publications, 1990 [orig. pub. 1881]), 13.

If we neglect the command of 1 Timothy 4:16—if we fail to watch our life closely, carefully, and uncompromisingly—negative consequences are inevitable for ourselves, our family, our pastoral team, and our church. A marked or prolonged inattention to personal holiness in a pastor is a grave matter that must be addressed. At Sovereign Grace Ministries we have sought to apply this passage in relation to the pastors of our local churches. We believe that the biblical requirement for a pastor is not flawless character but mature character. We are all progressively growing in godliness. A pastor who recognizes an area of immaturity and takes specific action towards change demonstrates close attention to his life and doctrine. Likewise, if a particular instance of nondisqualifying sin occurs in a pastor's life, but he genuinely repents before God and the appropriate individuals, this also honors the passage we are examining.

There are, of course, some sins that are particularly serious, both in the effect they have upon others and what they reveal about the condition of the heart. Even a single instance of sins such as sexual immorality, financial impropriety, violent behavior, and others would automatically disqualify a man from pastoral ministry. In addition to such grave instances of sin, a serious, ongoing pattern of disobedient deviation from biblical requirements in the life of a pastor can also be disqualifying.

For example, a single lustful look quickly confessed and repented of is part of growing maturity. However, a pattern of pornography could be disqualifying. Similarly, an isolated instance of lying speech promptly brought into the light is evidence of ongoing sanctification. Repeated examples of deceptive behavior, on the other hand, call into question a pastor's trustworthiness. Likewise, an outburst of irritation immediately regretted and repented of is proof the Holy Spirit is at work. But a reputation for anger is not consistent with the biblical requirements for a pastor.

Where such patterns of sin exist, we believe that genuine care for a pastor and a church involves a corrective process. Of course, this must be administered with all humility, gentleness, and patience. Occasions requiring the loving confrontation of a pastor in sin have been among the most difficult and painful of my ministry experience. But in the end, the corrective process has normally produced God-glorifying and fruitful outcomes in a pastor's life, family, and church.

Let me give you one illustration from Covenant Life Church, where I had the privilege to pastor for more than twenty-seven years. In this case, we began a process of discipline and restriction of ministry for one of our pastors, because over a period of years he had not watched certain areas of his life closely. Despite the ongoing care and correction of his friends in ministry, he persisted in serious patterns of pride and laziness. Consequently, his godly example was compromised. This man has humbly granted me permission to relate his story and share the following portions of his written confession.

> My pride has brought me to this place. Pride shows itself in many ways. For me it has been self-sufficiency, self-reliance, and self-righteousness and a craving for honor and admiration. . . . My small group faithfully pointed out these things over the years, but I listened and applied their counsel only sporadically. I brought an incomplete picture to my friends who had concerns. . . . And when they brought those concerns, I wouldn't follow up faithfully with questions or ask for their help. This amounts to stubborn resistance. At times when the situation became egregious I would get busy, but when the crisis died down, I reverted to former patterns of laziness and pride. . . . On one occasion . . . as things deteriorated, my small group questioned whether I was really taking things seriously. Of course, I was sure I was. But they went around the room one by one and, to a man, all six of them said "We don't think you are." I was tempted to argue with this assessment. Sadly, that has been my pattern for many years. I would listen and put on an out-

ward show of concurrence. But when I disagreed, I would be comfortable in my own assessment and dismissive of the concerns of others. . . . *Six people saying one thing,* and I was still inclined to trust my own assessment. That's serious stubbornness! "The way of a fool seems right to him, but a wise man listens to advice" (Prov. 12:15 NIV).

I'm happy to report that the process of discipline in his life has resulted in a fruitful outcome. I'm so grateful for his repentance and humility and the subsequent change in his life. Nevertheless, addressing my friend's sin and caring for his soul included many difficult and painful moments for the pastoral team at Covenant Life Church. The experience, while sobering for us all, served as a powerful reminder of the importance of paying constant, careful attention to our lives. Watch your life; watch it closely.

The War Within Never Ends

We often fail to watch our lives closely because we forget that within our heart lies a dangerous enemy, an enemy dead-set against the pursuit of God and godliness. Paul vividly describes the reality of our spiritual conflict: "For the desires of the flesh are against the Spirit, and the desires of the Spirit are against the flesh, for these are opposed to each other, to keep you from doing the things you want to do" (Gal. 5:17). This is no pre-conversion description of a non-Christian; rather, it is a post-conversion description of the war within a regenerated heart. Indwelling sin, or remaining sin, is present in each of us. It is tenacious, destructive, and unremitting in its opposition to grace. We are commanded to keep a close watch on our lives precisely because of this ever-active enemy within.

No one has taught me more about indwelling sin than John Owen. I agree with what I once heard J. I. Packer say: "Owen showed me that there is far more than I had ever known both to indwelling sin in believers and God's gracious work of sanctification. Owen searched me to the root of my being and he brought God close to me. No one probes the depths of the human heart with such grace, authority, and skill as Owen." So let us listen to the good Puritan that we might benefit from his gracious and skillful probing:

> Many men live in the dark to themselves all their days; whatever else they know, they know not themselves. They know their outward estates, how rich they are, and the condition of their bodies as to health and sickness they are careful to examine; but as to their inward man, and their principles as to God and eternity, they know little or nothing of themselves. Indeed, few labor to grow wise in this matter, few study themselves as they ought, are acquainted with the evil of their own hearts as they ought; on which yet the whole course of their obedience, and consequently of their eternal condition, doth depend.[4]

Do you labor to grow wise about your soul? Do you study yourself as you ought? For Owen is surely right that the whole course of our eternal condition depends upon it. There is no pastoral privilege in relation to sin, no suspension of sin's temptations or exemption from its effects for men in the ministry; there is only a heightened responsibility to consistently fight and weaken sin—and more serious consequences for the pastor who fails to do so (James 3:1). Never imagine for a moment that God will overlook your sin because of the importance of your role. Imagining you are exempt is a grave mistake.

Because you have an opponent that never rests, your war never ends. Therefore, if you do not watch your heart and life closely, you are surely in danger. If you don't watch, you will weaken. So are

---

[4] John Owen, "Indwelling Sin," in *The Works of John Owen* (Edinburgh: Banner of Truth, 1967), 6:162.

you watching? Are you watching closely? Heart work is certainly hard work; it's humbling work, but it's necessary work because sin is always at work. And that, my friends, is why we need one another.

We Can't Fight the War Alone

If you're like me, you have no problem acknowledging pervasive depravity as a broad doctrinal category. How hard is it to admit that you are one of nearly seven billion living sinners who in terms of their fallen nature are basically all in the same boat? Sin of that sort—generalized, homogenized, the universal bottom line—isn't very embarrassing, is it? No, it's the specific, personal expressions of my own depravity that I have difficulty admitting.

Although it is not easy to confess my sin to others specifically, the reality is that I cannot watch myself by myself. I need others. I need the discerning eyes of friends on my heart and life to fulfill this command. God in his wisdom has designed it so. If left to myself, my discernment of sin would be deficient and my growth in godliness limited. I would in fact resemble the man described in the following story:

> As I sat with my family at a local breakfast establishment, I noticed a finely dressed man at an adjacent table: his Armani suit and stiffly pressed shirt coordinated perfectly with a power tie. His wing-tip shoes sparkled from a recent shine; every hair was in place, including his perfectly groomed moustache. The man sat alone eating a bagel as he prepared for a meeting. As he reviewed the papers before him, he appeared nervous, glancing frequently at his Rolex watch. It was obvious he had an important meeting ahead. The man stood up and I watched as he straightened his tie and prepared to leave. Immediately I noticed a blob of cream cheese attached to his finely groomed moustache. He was about to go into the world, dressed in his finest, with cream cheese on his face. I thought of the business meet-

ing he was about to attend. Who would tell him? Should I? What if no one did?[5]

As you and I walk through life, no matter how closely we watch ourselves, we are acquiring fresh blobs of cream cheese on our faces. We all have "cream cheese" moments. Let me tell you about one of many such moments in my life.

It happened as I was meeting one day with the small group of men who take responsibility to care for my soul. I planned to share with them two areas of sin from the previous week. While fairly certain that I needed help understanding the second pattern of sin, I considered the first something of a formality. I desired to confess it in order to be transparent, but the nature and root of the sin seemed clear to me. I wanted to spend minimal time on that first sin so we could have ample opportunity to examine the second.

So I informed the men about the first sin, which is a pattern of complaining in my life. As I had been preparing to speak at a conference recently, a number of small, unexpected trials had come my way. In pride I thought, "These inconveniences shouldn't be happening to me. I'm busy preparing to serve God's people." I failed to remember that God has not promised to protect me from trial or suspend his work of sanctification when I am preparing a message. The root of this sinful complaining, I told them, was pride. I explained that I had already confessed this sin to God and asked for his forgiveness; but before I could move on to the second sin, one of the men asked a question about my complaining. I answered, and then someone asked a second question. As additional questions were raised, I initially feigned a patient response, but I was perplexed. Hadn't I been clear? The root of complain-

---

[5] Attributed to Pastor James R. Needham in an illustration from www.preachingtoday.com (2004). See C. J. Mahaney, *Humility: True Greatness* (Sisters, OR: Multnomah, 2005), 125.

ing is obviously pride, which I had confessed to God and to them, so why all these questions?

By outward appearances I was trying to humble myself—taking notes, making eye contact, nodding, and muttering "hmm" in all the right places—but the façade was becoming difficult to maintain. "Do you think there might be anything else at the root of this sin?" someone asked. That's when I launched into a mini-teaching on the nature of pride and how it lies at the very heart of so many of our sins. I was irritated with my friends' questions, and my responses were not humble.

You see, I fully expected to receive appreciation and commendation for the humility of my confession and the insightful accuracy of my self-analysis—not a succession of inquiries. Where did this group of theological ignoramuses come from? What happened to my intelligent and discerning friends? But, no, these were the same guys—wise and godly men—and they weren't convinced that I really understood the sin underlying my complaining. As we continued to talk, much more sin was revealed than I had originally perceived.

I learned a lot that day. I learned that I tend to trust my own discernment about my sin. I learned that sin had deceived and blinded me in this area. This was obvious to them yet invisible to me. There was, in effect, a big blob of cream cheese on my face. And I had no clue. But my friends saw it, and they were kindly trying to help me wipe it away. Because I can often see other people's sin clearly, I assume that I can see *my* sin clearly. But it doesn't work that way. My own sin has an unusual ability to blind me, almost as if it never existed. The sin of a sinner is self-deceiving.

I love the way Paul Tripp unfolds this truth in his excellent book *Instruments in the Redeemer's Hands*:

> Since each of us still has sin remaining in us, we will have pockets of spiritual blindness. Our most important vision system is

not our physical eyes. We can be physically blind and live quite well. But when we are spiritually blind, we cannot live as God intended. Physically blind people are always aware of their deficit and spend much of their lives learning to live with its limitations. But the Bible says that we can be spiritually blind and yet think that we see quite well. We even get offended when people act as if they see us better than we see ourselves! The reality of spiritual blindness has important implications for the Christian community. The Hebrews passage [Hebrews 3:13] clearly teaches that personal insight is the product of community. I need you in order to really see and know myself. Otherwise, I will listen to my own arguments, believe my own lies, and buy into my own delusions. My self-perception is as accurate as a carnival mirror. If I am going to see myself clearly, I need you to hold the mirror of God's Word in front of me."[6]

Since my self-perception is as accurate as a carnival mirror, I need to *ask* others to hold up the mirror of God's Word. I need to humbly, but diligently and aggressively, *seek out* appropriate individuals and implore them to help me see my sin. And I must honestly inform them about my temptations and sins instead of presenting a carefully edited or flattering version of myself. If I limit the evaluation of myself to myself, I will simply deceive myself—I certainly won't be fooling anybody else!

Each of us can safely assume that we have cream cheese on our face, which our wives and close friends clearly see. They have observations about our character but may be reluctant to share their concerns. Normally, to uncover these insights we must ask for them and then create an unhurried context in which they might be thoroughly explained and clearly understood. We must not wait until there is a crisis in our lives, our marriages, or our parenting before we involve others in the process. For the sake of our wives, for the sake of our children, for the sake of the Savior, and those

[6] Paul David Tripp, *Instruments in the Redeemer's Hands* (Phillipsburg, NJ: P&R, 2002), 54.

in our churches for whom he died, let us aggressively pursue the observations of others. What an opportunity this presents to put sin to death! By the very act of asking for observations, we can deal a blow to pride. What an excellent way to watch our life closely.

So let's get practical. Let me recommend that you present your wife with a gift in the form of a question. Sit down with her in some pleasant environment free from distractions and with ample time for a lengthy conversation. Then ask her, "What are three areas of character in which you would most like to see me grow by the grace of God?"

Then listen, very closely and very patiently. This is likely to be a "cream cheese" moment for you, so take notes. Speak only to draw out further observations and to express your appreciation for her thoughts. This is no time for you to raise objections, make rationalizations, or dismiss or challenge her observations. You need your wife like you need no one else, because she sees you like no one else. Recognize that you are undoubtedly blind to some of your sin and receive her insights with gratitude.

Next, ask the same question of the men on your pastoral team, or, if you serve alone, with two or three men whom you respect for their godly character and whom you trust to care for your soul. Again, welcome every response and abstain from all explanation and justification of your actions. Take more notes. Then ask them these additional questions: Do I confess specific instances of sin? Do I make you aware of my present temptations and my patterns of sin? Am I easy to correct? You have nothing to lose and everything to gain by asking. Your humility will result in an experience of God's grace (James 4:6). Their observations will help you grow, and your example will provoke others to greater godliness.

Finally, don't keep private the fight with sin. Acknowledge to your congregation your daily battle with sin. Don't allow the church to assume erroneously that you are above those temptations common to man. Where appropriate, inform them from the pulpit of your temptations and sins. Regularly use personal illustrations of your failings when making application in your sermons. Make sure the members of your congregation know that the pastoral team is aware of your current temptations and is providing care for your soul.

We can't fight the war alone. We can't watch ourselves by ourselves. But if we aggressively pursue the observations of our wife, our pastoral team, and even the members of our church, we will be fulfilling the mandate of 1 Timothy 4:16. By the grace of God and with the help of others, we can watch our lives closely.

A Model for Your Consideration

In our ministry we have sought to establish a set of practices whereby pastors can help one another to watch their lives closely. The fruit from these practices has been immeasurable. While I am not recommending a strict emulation of our model, I do strongly exhort every pastoral team to create and implement a clearly defined structure for the application of 1 Timothy 4:16. Without such structure, obedience to this command will surely take a back seat to the daily demands of life and ministry responsibilities. This highest responsibility—to watch your life—will get lost in the shuffle.

It all begins at the local church level. In Covenant Life, pastoral teams and their wives meet together in small groups for the purpose of watching one another's lives closely. We meet monthly as a small group of couples, plus there are two separate monthly meetings— one for the men in pastoral ministry and another for their wives. Much interaction also occurs outside of these meetings. The primary purpose of each meeting is growth in godliness. This is not a time to evaluate the church or discuss strategic direction. The focus is intentionally narrow: to watch ourselves closely and to welcome the eyes of our friends upon our hearts and lives.

Additionally, we schedule a three-day retreat each year. This provides an unhurried atmosphere in which we can give undivided attention to each couple on the pastoral team. Again, the focus is care for one another and growth in godliness, with special concentration on marriage and parenting.

In my experience, few practices have proven more helpful than the ones I've just described. Three decades of counseling, encouraging, correcting, and praying for one another have been absolutely indispensable to our efforts to obey 1 Timothy 4:16.

So I will ask you directly: Are you watching closely? Are you persisting? Were you more diligent about matters of your heart early in your ministry yet less concerned now? Are you informing your wife and fellow pastors about your present temptations and sins, or are you attempting to hide a certain sin from those closest to you? Are you convicted even as you read these words?

If so, please humble yourself immediately before God and the appropriate individuals by acknowledging your specific sins. To those who arrogantly presume they can successfully hide their sin, Scripture warns, "Whoever conceals his transgressions will not prosper." However, this verse also contains a wonderful promise for the man who humbly admits his sins: "but he who confesses and forsakes them will obtain mercy" (Prov. 28:13).

Given the continual presence of indwelling sin, our tendency to self-deception, and the eternal stakes for ourselves and our congregations, Paul's exhortation should never be far from our minds. "Watch your life." Watch it closely. Watch it continuously. Until your dying breath, never stop watching your life.

Watch Your Doctrine

Because the rest of this book aims to equip pastors in sound doctrine, there is little need for me to elaborate on that here. I simply want to accent one aspect of Paul's admonition. As we watch our doctrine, we must never forget that which is central to our doctrine: the gospel of Jesus Christ. If you fail to keep the gospel at the core of your life and ministry, you have ceased to watch your doctrine closely. "The preachers' commission," writes J. I. Packer, "is to declare the whole counsel of God; but the cross is the center of that counsel, and the Puritans knew that the traveler through the Bible landscape misses his way as soon as he loses sight of the hill called Calvary."[7]

In all our preaching, we must never lose sight of the hill called Calvary, where the Son of Man was killed in our place. Regardless of the text or topic at hand, there must be some view of Calvary in every sermon. Your congregation should experience the amazing and comforting sight of the crucified Savior each and every time you preach. They should anticipate the sight of Calvary in every sermon and rejoice when it comes into view, and all the more when the cross is not immediately obvious in the text. "Where is the hill?" they should be asking. "Where is that blessed hill on which our precious Savior died?" We should exalt Christ's finished work in our sermons so as to comfort the converted and convict the unbeliever.

Spurgeon's example should inspire us: "I received some years ago orders from my Master to stand at the foot of the cross until he comes. He has not come yet, but I mean to stand there until he does."[8] Let us stand with the prince of preachers, gentlemen. As we preach the whole counsel of God, let us keep the cross central. By doing so, we will indeed be watching our doctrine.

Watch the Savior Work

As we watch our life, and as we watch our doctrine—closely, persistently, and with the help of others—we can expect a most astonishing outcome. For at the end of 1 Timothy 4:16 is an unexpected promise: "Persist in this, for by so doing you will save both your-

[7] J. I. Packer, A Quest for Godliness (Wheaton, IL: Crossway, 1990), 286.
[8] C. H. Spurgeon, "The Old, Old Story," The Spurgeon Archive (http://www.spurgeon.org/sermons/0446.htm [accessed July 2006]).

self and your hearers." To be sure, Paul is not teaching self-atone-
ment, for we cannot and do not save ourselves. Instead, he is
accenting God-ordained human agency in the experience of salvation. It is in this seemingly curious phrase that we encounter the
effect of godly leadership.

God, who can do all things without assistance, has nevertheless
chosen to do some of his work through us. In commenting on this
verse George Knight writes, "Thus we see that the New Testament
speaks of human agents in addition to the ultimate and absolute
source, God himself."[9] R. C. H. Lenski notes, "God alone saves, yet
he saves by means, and it is thus that one who uses and applies
these means can very properly be said to save himself and others."[10]
Finally, Calvin comments, "Although salvation is God's gift alone,
yet human ministry is needed, as is here implied."[11]

Simply stated, God uses human ministry and godly leadership
as a means of grace. So as you and I obey the conditional elements
of verse 16 we may have every confidence that God will preserve us
and those whom we serve for that final day. Here's why: this
promise, like every promise of salvation found in Scripture, is guar-
anteed in and fulfilled by the finished work of the "one mediator
between God and men, the man Christ Jesus" (1 Tim. 2:5). Pause
and consider this as you face the daunting demands of pastoral
ministry. Who stands behind and guarantees the fruitfulness of
your labors? Our Mediator. What assures you that by your
"watching your life and doctrine," men and women will spend
eternity with God? The work of our Savior. What empowers your
close watching and diligent persistence? The cross of Christ.

Indeed, were it not for Christ's finished work, the burden of this

---

[9] George Knight III, *The Pastoral Epistles: A Commentary on the Greek Text* (Grand Rapids, MI: Eerdmans, 1992), 212.

[10] R. C. H. Lenski, *The Interpretation of St. Paul's Epistles to the Colossians, to the Thessalonians, to Timothy, to Titus, and to Philemon* (Minneapolis: Augsburg, 1964), 650.

[11] Donald Guthrie, *The Pastoral Epistles,* Tyndale New Testament Commentaries (Grand Rapids, MI: Eerdmans, 1984), 99.

verse would be too much to bear. But because of the Savior, you can have hope for ultimate fruitfulness in your pastoral ministry. You can have hope that your life will increasingly reflect the transforming effects of the gospel. You can have hope that your preaching will faithfully proclaim your Savior. And you can have hope that your ministry will contribute to the preservation of yourself and the congregation under your care. As you watch your life, and as you watch your doctrine, you can be confident that *you will see the Savior work.*

CHAPTER 7

WHY I STILL PREACH THE BIBLE AFTER FORTY YEARS OF MINISTRY

John MacArthur

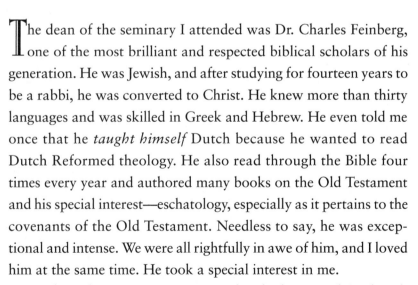

The dean of the seminary I attended was Dr. Charles Feinberg, one of the most brilliant and respected biblical scholars of his generation. He was Jewish, and after studying for fourteen years to be a rabbi, he was converted to Christ. He knew more than thirty languages and was skilled in Greek and Hebrew. He even told me once that he *taught himself* Dutch because he wanted to read Dutch Reformed theology. He also read through the Bible four times every year and authored many books on the Old Testament and his special interest—eschatology, especially as it pertains to the covenants of the Old Testament. Needless to say, he was exceptional and intense. We were all rightfully in awe of him, and I loved him at the same time. He took a special interest in me.

In those days, every seminary student had to preach in chapel. When my turn came, Dr. Feinberg assigned me to preach on 2 Samuel 7, the great text on the Davidic covenant and one of his favorites. My sermon was probably an acceptable model of structural craftsmanship. It had a zinger for a beginning and a zapper at the end. It would have been a great success, too—if it hadn't been for my failure to explain the true significance of the text. I preached a *practical* message that was only superficially related to the intent of the biblical text. In that passage, Nathan encourages David to build a house for the Lord, but God says in essence, "Wait a minute, you didn't check in. That's not the plan." So I preached about how important it is not to presume on God.

When I finished, I felt pretty good. The chapel audience seemed to have followed with interest, and I even thought I heard some murmurs of approval. But I really only cared about the opinion of one man—my mentor, Dr. Feinberg. The faculty sat behind us when we preached in chapel, filling out legal-sized criticism sheets during the student's sermon. After we preached, we stood at the door, and the faculty handed us their sheets as they left the room. The only sheet I wanted was Dr. Feinberg's.

He was at the end of the line, and I could see that he had folded his sheet very small and tight. When he handed it to me, he did not even look at my face. He kept his eyes straight down and walked firmly past. That was not a good sign. So at my first opportunity, I unfolded his paper. I was eager to read his feedback, hoping desperately that he would be impressed with my sermon.

To be sure, I expected some constructive criticism. But the few bold red words that stared back at me were *much* worse than anything I had prepared myself for. He had completely ignored all the suggested categories and scoring helps that were printed on the sheet. Instead, he wrote across the page in bold red letters a one-line critique that hit me like a hard punch to the solar plexus: "You missed the whole point of the passage." That is the worst possible mistake any preacher could make—but especially in front of someone like Dr. Feinberg.

Like many young preachers, I had naïvely concerned myself with just about everything *except* getting the meaning of the text right. My preparation was focused on delivery, gestures, anecdotes, the right mix of humor and illustrative material, the alliteration of my main points, and applicability. I had actually approached the theology of the passage itself almost as an afterthought.

Later that day, I received a message instructing me to go to Dr. Feinberg's office. When I got there, he was sitting at his desk, shaking his head in disappointment. "How could you? How *could* you? That passage presents the Davidic covenant culminating in the Messiah and his glorious kingdom—and you talked about 'not presuming on God' in our personal day-to-day choices. That would have been a fine admonition to preach from Numbers 15:30–31 or Psalm 19:13, but you can't reduce 2 Samuel 7 to *that!* You missed the entire point of the passage, and it's one of the greatest of all Old Testament passages. Don't ever do that again."

He never said another word about it to me, but that incident hit me like a sledgehammer. In fact, it was the deepest single impression I ever received in seminary. *Never miss the point of the passage.* To this day, when I come to the text each week and begin to study its richness and depth, I can still hear Dr. Feinberg's heartfelt admonition ringing in my ears. If you don't have the *meaning* of Scripture, you do not have the Word of God at all. If you miss the true sense of what God has said, you are not actually preaching God's Word! That reality has compelled me for nearly forty years of preaching.

During these years, I've seen numerous evangelical trends come and go. Whether it's a new way of doing church or the latest self-help book, contemporary Christian fads are transient by their very nature. Pastors who embrace these fads, usually in an attempt to be culturally relevant, inevitably find themselves neglecting the exposition of God's Word, looking for something else, desperately trying to keep up with whatever is supposedly cutting edge. Many preachers in the current generation seem to find it hard to resist the temptation to approach ministry that way. After all, the endless parade of fads is going in the same direction that the mainstream of the evangelical movement is flowing. Adapting your ministry to keep up with cultural and ecclesiastical fads is precisely what most books on pastoral ministry advocate. It's the pattern many of evangelicalism's best-known pastors have followed. It's even what most seminaries nowadays teach their students.

But for some forty years now, I have resisted and opposed all those trends. And one of the main things that still constrains me is Dr. Feinberg's admonition to a second-year seminary student—which continually echoes in my head as I prepare my sermons—reminding me to keep focused on the main thing, to concentrate on getting the meaning of Scripture right, and to consume my energies preaching the Word of God as accurately and as faithfully as possible.

Sadly and ironically, in its attempt to achieve cultural relevance, mainstream evangelicalism has become essentially irrelevant. As Os Guinness points out, the seductive promise of *relevance* is, in reality, the road to irrelevance.[1] When the church markets itself like the world, the distinctiveness of its message is lost and the gospel is irretrievably compromised. The entertainment value may be high, attracting throngs each week, but the eternal value is conspicuously absent, as those same people go home unchallenged and unchanged. Besides, the quest for cultural relevance is contrary to everything Scripture teaches about church ministry. Preachers are called to preach the word of God, unfiltered by notions of political correctness, undiluted by the preacher's own ideas, and unadapted to the spirit of the age.

That is how I have approached ministry from the beginning. My father was a pastor, and when I first told him years ago that I believed God was calling me to a life of ministry, he gave me a Bible in which he had inscribed these words of encouragement: "Preach the Word!" That simple statement became the compelling stimu-

---

[1] See Os Guinness, *Dining with the Devil* (Grand Rapids: Baker, 1993), 64–67.

lus in my heart. It is the one thing I have endeavored to do above all else in my ministry: preach the correct interpretation of the Word, which yields sound theology.

Pastors today face relentless pressure to do everything *but* that. They are encouraged to be storytellers, comedians, psychologists, or motivational speakers. They are warned to steer clear of topics that people find unpleasant. Many have given up biblical preaching in favor of shallow talks designed to make people feel good. Some have even replaced preaching with drama and other forms of staged entertainment.

But the pastor whose passion is biblical and doctrinal has only one option: "Preach the word; be ready in season and out of season; reprove, rebuke, exhort, with great patience and instruction" (2 Tim. 4:2).[2] When Paul wrote those words to Timothy, he added this prophetic warning: "The time will come when they will not endure sound doctrine; but after their own lusts shall they heap to themselves teachers, having itching ears; and they shall turn away their ears from the truth" (vv. 3–4 KJV).

Clearly there was no room in Paul's philosophy of ministry for the give-people-what-they-want theory that is so prevalent today. He was no "man pleaser" (Gal. 1:10; Eph. 6:6). He did not urge Timothy to conduct a survey to find out what his people wanted. He commanded him to preach the Word—faithfully, reprovingly, and patiently.

In fact, far from urging Timothy to devise a ministry that would garner accolades from the world, Paul warned the young pastor about suffering and hardship! Paul was not telling Timothy how to be *successful*; he was encouraging him to follow the divine standard. He was not advising him to pursue prosperity, power, prominence, popularity, or any of the other worldly notions of suc-

---

[2] Unless otherwise noted, Scripture references in this chapter are taken from *The New American Standard Bible* (NASB).

cess. He was urging the young pastor to be *biblical*—regardless of the consequences.

Expository preaching that is theological is not easy. The stringent discipline required to interpret Scripture accurately is a constant burden, and the message we are required to proclaim is often offensive. Christ himself is a stone of stumbling and a rock of offense (Rom. 9:33; 1 Pet. 2:8). The message of the cross is a stumbling block to some (1 Cor. 1:23; Gal. 5:11) and mere foolishness to others (1 Cor. 1:23).

But we are never permitted to trim the message or tailor it to people's preferences. Paul made this clear to Timothy at the end of chapter 3: "*All Scripture* is inspired by God and profitable for teaching, for reproof, for correction, for training in righteousness" (2 Tim. 3:16). This is the Word to be preached: the whole counsel of God (cf. Acts 20:27).

In chapter 1 Paul had told Timothy, "Retain the standard of sound words which you have heard from me" (v. 13). He was speaking of the revealed words of Scripture—all of it. He urged Timothy to "Guard . . . the treasure which has been entrusted to you" (v. 14). Then in chapter 2 he told him to study the Word and handle it accurately (v. 15). He then brings the epistle to its summit by urging him to proclaim God's Word no matter what. So the entire task of the faithful minister revolves around the Word of God—guarding it, studying it, and proclaiming it.

In Colossians 1 the apostle Paul, describing his own ministry philosophy, writes, "Of this church I was made a minister according to the stewardship from God bestowed on me for your benefit, *so that I might fully carry out the preaching of the word of God*" (v. 25). In 1 Corinthians he goes a step further: "When I came to you, brethren, I did not come with superiority of speech or of wisdom, proclaiming to you the testimony of God. For I determined to know nothing among you except Jesus Christ, and Him crucified" (2:1–2). In other words, his goal as a preacher was not to entertain people with his rhetorical style, or to amuse them with cleverness, humor, novel insights, or sophisticated methodology. He simply preached Christ crucified.

Faithfully preaching and teaching the Word *must* be the very heart of our ministry philosophy. Any other approach replaces the voice of God with human wisdom. Philosophy, politics, humor, psychology, homespun advice, and personal opinion can never accomplish what the Word of God does. Those things may be interesting, informative, entertaining, and sometimes even helpful—but they are not the business of the church. The preacher's task is not to be a conduit for human wisdom; he is God's voice to speak to the congregation. No human message comes with the stamp of divine authority—only the Word of God. How dare any preacher substitute another message?

I frankly do not understand preachers who are willing to abdicate this solemn privilege. Why should we proclaim the wisdom of men when we have the privilege of preaching the Word of God?

Ten Reasons to Preach the Word of God

With that in mind, below are ten reasons I'm still preaching the Bible after forty years of ministry. This is not an exhaustive list, but I trust it will encourage ministers to be faithful to proclaim the Word of God to the people of God through the power of the Spirit of God.

1) Because the Message of God's Word Is Timeless and Truly Powerful

A primary reason I still preach the Bible is that this alone is God's eternal and divinely empowered message. Thus it is both timeless and truly powerful. Forty years of ministry (or *any* finite number for that matter) could never begin to exhaust it, either in terms of its freshness and richness, its depth of teaching, or its ability to impact lives. The Word of God is timeless because its Author is timeless—and no matter how the culture changes, God's message never changes.

Scripture is powerful because, unlike man-made programs and solutions which never really get below the surface, the Bible is empowered by God himself. That's why it is able to transform people in the deepest reaches of their hearts. Hence, I preach the Bible because this ancient book, in which the knowledge of God is revealed, contains all that people need for every aspect of life and godliness (2 Pet. 1:3). That reality defines *true* relevance, and that is exactly why Paul told Timothy to preach the Word in season and out of season.

Let's face it—in our generation, the Word is "out of season." The market-driven philosophy currently in vogue says that plainly declaring biblical truth is outmoded and ineffective in this climate of postmodernism. Biblical exposition and theology are seen as antiquated and extraneous. Churchgoers don't want to be preached to anymore, according to this philosophy. It acts on the belief that Generation Y won't just sit in the pew while someone up front preaches at them; they are products of a media-driven generation, and they need a church experience that will satisfy them on their own terms by giving them what they are used to. Meanwhile, Emergent leaders are insisting that the Scripture is unclear as to its meaning anyway.

We are definitely in an "out of season" time, which is exactly what the Holy Spirit anticipated when he inspired this mandate. But the modern evangelical misunderstanding of this text seems to indicate that many church leaders nowadays think it means "preach the Word *in season,* period, and let people tell you when it's in season."

There have always been men in the pulpit who gather crowds because they are gifted orators, interesting storytellers, entertaining speakers, dynamic personalities, shrewd crowd-manipulators, rousing speechmakers, popular politicians, or erudite scholars. Such preaching may be *popular*, but it is not necessarily *powerful*. No one can preach with power who does not preach *the Word*. And no faithful preacher will water down or neglect the whole counsel of God. Proclaiming the Word—all of it—is the pastor's calling.

2) Because God's Word Is the Good News of Salvation

A second reason to preach the Word is that Scripture alone unfolds God's plan of salvation. As Peter said to Jesus, "To whom [else] shall we go? You have words of eternal life" (John 6:68). Why would I ever go anywhere else for spiritual answers than to the inspired revelation of Jesus Christ? Scripture reveals "the mind of Christ" (1 Cor. 2:16). I certainly don't have the words of life; nor does anyone else. Only he does.

The Bible makes it clear that, no matter what people's *felt* needs may be, their *real* need is for forgiveness and salvation from sin so as to escape eternal hell and enter the bliss of heaven. A fulfilled life, a happy marriage, a loving friendship, a successful career—those "needs" pale in comparison with the eternal issue facing every human being. It does not make any sense, then, for pastors to focus all of their energies on temporal surface attitudes while leaving the most profound eternal needs unaddressed. Besides, a true understanding of eternal life changes how we react to the passing troubles of this life. Yet, this is precisely what pastors do when they abandon the Bible for some man-made, market-driven ministry strategy.

The Bible also makes it clear that genuine belief includes more than just mental assent (see James 2:19). Biblical faith is more than just a profession of faith; it is a change of allegiance—from the mastery of sin to the lordship of Christ. As a preacher, it certainly would be convenient for me to preach a gospel that says: "If you've ever made a profession of faith in Jesus, then you're saved, even if there's nothing in your life to validate that claim." But I can't do that, because that's not the true gospel. The true gospel repeatedly commands unbelievers to repent (Matt. 4:17; 11:20–21; Mark 6:12; Luke 5:32; 13:3, 5; 15:7, 10; 24:47; Acts 2:38; 3:19; 11:18; 17:30; 20:21; 2 Cor. 7:9–10; 2 Tim. 2:25) and tells us that, "If we say that we have fellowship with Him and yet walk in the darkness, we lie and do not practice the truth" (1 John 1:6). It urges us to "test yourselves to see if you are in the faith" (2 Cor. 13:5), and reminds us that "You will know them by their fruits" (Matt. 7:16–18; cf. Luke 6:43–44). So I preach the Bible because I want to make sure I'm preaching the true gospel and not a gospel of my own imagination.

When I came out of seminary, I really did not expect to fight the battles I have fought over the last four decades. I knew I would face some different paradigms of ministry and opinions about ecclesiology. I understood that there were various views of eschatology and of biblical inspiration, etc. But I never thought I would spend most of my life on the broader evangelical front defending the biblical gospel and sound doctrine from so-called believers who attempted to undermine both. The Word of God, rightly interpreted, defines the truth.

3) Because God's Word Sets Forth Divine Truth with Clarity and Certainty

I preach the Word of God because it is understandable. God revealed his Word in such a way that it can be comprehended with clarity (cf. Ps. 119:105, 130). If he had not done so, the Bible would no longer serve as an objective standard for life, since it could not be understood in a straightforward sense. Yet, because he has revealed his Word in a way that is universally comprehensible, all men are accountable to it.

If the clarity of Scripture is denied, the certainty of any biblical doctrine must also be rejected, since we can no longer be sure that the Bible actually means what it says. Once doctrinal certainty grounded in biblical authority is dismissed, personal convictions must also be discarded, since they no longer have any firm foundation. And if personal convictions disappear, spiritual community will also vanish, since true fellowship necessarily begins with shared doctrines and convictions.

A healthy church is one that is motivated by a common affection for God and his Word and really knows what it is to love one another. That affection, both for God and for others, arises out of the confidence that the Bible is true, that it is absolute, and that it can be understood.

Scripture *is* clear. Deny that simple fact and you forfeit all confidence and conviction. No wonder evangelicals who have drifted away from the centrality of Scripture seem to lack certainty and clarity about *anything*. Careful exegesis and doctrinal precision are inevitable casualties of postmodern uncertainty, too. Consider this shocking comment from a supposedly conservative minister: "If there is a foundation in Christian theology, and I believe that there must be, then it is not found in the Church, Scripture, tradition or culture. . . . Theology must be a humble human attempt to 'hear him'—never about rational approaches to texts."[3] That is an amazing statement. It is ludicrous. How can we truly "hear him," meaning God, unless we go to the place he has spoken—his Word? The only way I can ever be certain about *anything* is to approach every biblical text with a careful, rational, discerning mind to hear and understand accurately what God is saying. Take that away, and what basis is there for certainty about *any* truth?

Indeed, a popular writer in the Emergent movement says, "Certainty is overrated."[4] In one of his books, he writes, "I have

---

[3] John Armstrong, "How I Changed My Mind: Theological Method," *Viewpoint* (Sep–Oct 2003): 4. In a follow-up on this subject at his weblog, Armstrong likens Christians who have "a high level of certitude" to dictators and tyrants. That article is titled, "Certitude Can Be Idolatrous" (June 30, 2005) http://johnharmstrong.com/.

[4] Brian McLaren, cited in Greg Warner, "Brian McLaren," *FaithWorks* (http://www.faithworks.com/archives/brian_mclaren.htm).

gone out of my way to be provocative, mischievous, and unclear, reflecting my belief that clarity is sometimes overrated, and that shock, obscurity, playfulness, and intrigue (carefully articulated) often stimulate more thought than clarity."[5] The wife of a leading pastor in the Emerging trend says, "I grew up thinking that we've figured out the Bible, that we knew what it means. *Now I have no idea what most of it means.* And yet I feel like life is big again—like life used to be black and white, and now it's in color [emphasis added]."[6] And so we often hear of the new hermeneutic, grossly mislabeled as the "hermeneutics of humility," which essentially says, "I'm far too humble to say I know what the Bible means by what it says, and anybody who claims to know what it means is arrogant."

But what's more arrogant than claiming God has not spoken clearly enough for us to understand? When I preach, one response that always pleases me most is, "The message was clear." Clarity is critical and basic. Ambiguity is deadly and produces nothing. People who think the truth itself is ambiguous don't know where to turn for salvation. They can't be sanctified. They don't find comfort. We get *nothing* from ambiguity except confusion. Clarity is the desired result of a good understanding of the biblical text. If a preacher is not clear to his hearers, it is likely because he is not yet clear in his own mind. That means more diligent study is required.

When I started in ministry, I committed myself to expository preaching, just explaining the Bible, because I knew that there was nothing I could say that was anywhere near as important as what God had to say. The real goal of my ministry has always been to keep my opinions out of it as much as possible—to get the meaning of the passage right and to make it clear to my hearers. Pastors need to remember from the very outset that when

---

[5] Brian McLaren, *A Generous Orthodoxy* (Grand Rapids, MI: Youth Specialties, 2004), 23.
[6] Kristen Bell, wife of Rob Bell. Cited by Andy Crouch, "The Emergent Mystique," *Christianity Today* (November 2004).

they go into a pulpit, they are there to explain the Word of the living God with clarity and precision, not to impress people with their own cleverness, or to amuse them with human opinions.

The Word of God is clear, and when I explain it accurately to my people, they understand it. That understanding is the first and most essential point of expositional preaching, because people cannot believe or obey truth they don't understand, thus building their lives on the wisdom that comes from above. A clear understanding of God's Word forms the convictions that shape our lives and leads to deep affection for divine truth (Ps. 119:129–31; 19:10).

4) Because God's Word Stands as the Authoritative Self-revelation of God

Preaching the Bible establishes the authority of God over the mind and the soul. When we preach the Word of God, our people understand who has sovereignty over their souls—it is God alone who reigns over their thoughts and their actions. I never want to be guilty of giving people the illusion that they have heard from God when in fact they have only heard from me. When I step into the pulpit, the expectation is that I'm the messenger of God. I speak on *his* behalf, not my own.

I remember having dinner with the owner of a nationally known newspaper, who, although not a believer, had come to our church out of curiosity. He asked me, "Why don't you ever give your opinion about anything?"

I responded by asking him: "Do you really need another opinion? You have a newspaper full of opinions every day, but as a pastor, I'm not called to give my opinion. I'm here to represent the Word of the living God. I have no desire to write my own opinion column, but if you would be willing to give me a column where I can express what God says on all these issues, I'd be glad to do that." Needless to say, he didn't take me up on that offer. But I think he understood my point.

As ambassadors for God, our task is not to promote our own ideas but rather to represent our King rightly. That means that all we should be doing is bringing the revealed truth of God to bear on the minds of men. Even our *thinking* has to be biblical. My prayer is that what Spurgeon said of Bunyan might be true of us today: "Why, this man is a living Bible! Prick him anywhere; his blood is Bibline, the very essence of the Bible flows from him. He cannot speak without quoting a text, for his very soul is full of the Word of God."[7] Simply put, we should be the voice of God on every issue in every place and era.

5) Because God's Word Exalts Christ as the Head of His Church

Expository preaching exalts the lordship of Christ over his church. The headship of Christ is surely one of the most assaulted and least understood doctrines in church history, including today. The doctrine itself has sailed down to us on a sea of blood due to long-standing conflict over the issue between the Reformers and the Roman Catholic Church. Catholics insist the pope is the head of the church, and the Roman church anathematizes those who deny that claim. Many Reformers lost their lives defending the belief that only Christ is Head of the church.

Yet, today, even the Protestant landscape is dotted with pastors who act as though they are the head of their church. Their mutiny against the true Head of the church is seen most clearly in their deliberate de-emphasis of his Word. By sidelining the Scriptures they are, in essence, silencing the voice of God in the church. After all, to take the Bible out of the church is to revolt against the church's one rightful Head. Conversely, to bring the Word of Christ

---

[7] Charles Spurgeon, "The Last Words of Christ on the Cross," No. 2644, Luke 23:46, *Metropolitan Tabernacle Pulpit*, Vol. 45.

to his people is to facilitate and exalt the headship of Christ over his church.

John Huss was one of the earliest Reformers who lost his life over this issue. On July 6, 1415, he was taken from his cell and dressed in priestly garments, of which he was then stripped one by one. He was tied to a stake and asked one last time to recant. When he refused, he was burned alive. His dying prayer was this: "Lord Jesus, it is for thee that I patiently endure this cruel death. I pray thee to have mercy on my enemies."[8] He literally died for the headship of Jesus Christ over the church.

Why did the Roman Catholic Church object to Huss's teachings? There were basically three issues in Huss's teaching that Rome opposed. First, Huss taught that all the church is made up of all predestined believers. That was in direct opposition to the Catholic view at the time, that the true church was embodied in the priesthood, and that the common people only *communed* with the church through the wafer. Second, Huss believed that the authority of the Bible was higher than the authority of the church; and third, along that same vein he taught that Jesus Christ himself was the Head of the church, not the pope or the priests. So it was an issue of authority. Huss said that Christ and his Word are sovereign in the church. Rome disagreed. And Huss was killed.

A hundred years later, Martin Luther came across a volume of sermons by John Huss. In reflecting on those sermons, Luther wrote, "I was overwhelmed with astonishment. I could not understand for what cause they had burnt so great a man, who explained the Scriptures with so much gravity and skill."[9] Both Huss's teaching and his life, particularly his unwillingness to compromise in the face of death, would become significant motivations for Luther and

---

[8] Cited in Mark Galli and Ted Olsen, eds., *131 Christians Everyone Should Know* (Nashville, TN: Broadman & Holman, 2000), 369–71.
[9] Ibid.

other later Reformers. Like Huss, they too would fight for the headship of Christ over his church. This was a key issue in the Reformation. And it is still a key issue today.

So who is the head of the church? It's certainly not me. I'm not the head of my church. I cringe at entrepreneurial ministry. As under-shepherds, pastors are responsible to serve the Chief Shepherd, not usurp his preeminence. When we preach the Word of God, we establish the Word of God over the mind and the soul, and thereby exalt the headship of Christ over his church. But to disregard Scripture is to disregard its Author, and doing that is nothing short of treachery.

6) Because God's Word Is the Means God Uses to Sanctify His People

A sixth reason to preach the Word of God is that it is the instrument the Spirit uses to save and sanctify. We are born again by the Word of truth. As Jesus said in John 17:17, "Sanctify them in the truth; your word is truth." All comfort, all encouragement, all nourishment, everything comes through the Word (cf. 1 Pet. 2:1–3) through which the Spirit works (compare Eph. 5:18–21 with Col. 3:16–17). The Word and the Spirit are really inseparable in terms of ministry. The Spirit is the one who breathed out the very Word of God through the human instruments who wrote it (2 Pet. 1:20–21), and it is his sword (Eph. 6:17).

Pastors need to ask themselves what they want from their churches. Do they want their people to be under the sovereign and blessed authority of God? Do they want them under the rule and headship of Jesus Christ? And do they want them in the midst of the powerful work of the Spirit of God? If they do, the appropriate course of action is straightforward: open the Bible and tell the people what it means and what doctrines it affirms, for the Spirit uses that truth to comfort and convict as it is conveyed to willing souls. It is even by the Word that he makes the unwilling, willing.

Preachers also are sanctified through the study and proclamation of God's Word. Even if I never preached another sermon, I would thank God every day of my life for the sanctifying grace that has come to me through the daily study of his precious Word. Pastors, then, should study to know God, not just to make sermons. For me, the greatest joy of preaching comes not in the final step of proclamation, but in the transformation of my own life as the truth pervades my thinking throughout the entire process. A sanctified preacher, known as such to his people, is a powerful instrument when he opens the Word.

So then, we preach the Word to others because it is the instrument God uses to save the lost and to sanctify his people. We also preach the Word to ourselves, because through our own study of Scripture we are likewise sanctified. And we take our sanctification seriously, lest after we have preached to others, we ourselves might somehow be disqualified (1 Cor. 9:27).

7) Because God's Word Rightly Informs Our Worship and Our Walk

Another reason I continue to do biblical exposition after all these years is that the Bible has a massive impact on the reality and genuineness of worship. I often tell young pastors at the outset of their ministries, "You have to go down if you're going to lead your people up." In other words, the degree to which your people will experience transcendent worship is directly related to the depth of their comprehension of divine truth. Those who understand the gospel the deepest are the ones who worship with the greatest exaltation and exhilaration.

Sadly, most churches are content to live in the flat land. The preacher never goes deep in his preaching so the people never go high in their worship. As a result, churches cannot express real worship that rises from a soul filled with the glory of the truth, so they replace it with emotional manipulation, smarmy tunes, and superstition. They call it worship, but it's really more an expression of feelings than an expression of true adoration rising from the mind that has grasped the depth of profound doctrine.

For me personally, the most important element in worship music is the lyrical content. The appropriate musical accompaniment should be suitable and memorable, but it is the words that carry the truth. When the words are teeming with rich theological life and biblical accuracy, they inform the mind and that launches a legitimate experience of glorifying God. But your people will not appreciate that type of profundity without the biblical background needed to understand the depth of the great realities about which they are singing. They have to be taught if they are to enjoy and express the true worship which God seeks (John 4:24).

Teaching the Bible expositionally also protects your people from error and carnality, so deadly not only to true worship but to a pure Christian walk. In some churches, pastors get up each week and do little "sermonettes for Christianettes," which are essentially short God-talks about self-help and positive feeling. But they do nothing for their people to protect them from error, sin, or temptation. The Bible speaks very pointedly about those so-called shepherds who fail to protect their sheep from spiritual harm (cf. John 10:12–13). Those who leave their sheep vulnerable to wolves are unfaithful shepherds. They have failed to impart any true knowledge of God; no doctrinal foundations have been laid; no deep soul work has been accomplished. Their communication style may be enjoyable, and their meetings may be full, but those pastors who do not faithfully proclaim the Word of God to their people are failing their sheep where it matters most. One day they will give an account to the Chief Shepherd for why they took such poor care of their flock (cf. 1 Pet. 5:1–4).

8) Because God's Word Brings Depth and Balance to My Ministry

A further benefit of consistent Bible exposition is that the preacher's faith and practice is tested by every text. Over the long haul, everything I have ever taught has had to survive the scrutiny of the Scriptures. Lord willing, I hope to teach through every verse of the New Testament (using the Old Testament as support and example) before the Lord calls me home. My life and my doctrine, then, have been radically shaped by the Word of God. I am being informed and refined by every verse in the New Testament with the support of the Old. My life and doctrine must stand the test of every single text.

In the big picture, preaching verse-by-verse, book-by-book, brings a divine balance to ministry. It keeps the preacher from leaving things out or from getting on a hobbyhorse and riding it to death. It forces him to deal with topics he might not naturally be drawn to if it were not for the fact that it is addressed in the next verse he is preaching. Put simply, it requires him to teach God's truth in the way God revealed it. And that's the best way to teach.

Some preachers allow their audience to determine what topic they will address. As one popular pastor has written:

> Adapt your style to fit your audience. . . . The ground we have in common with unbelievers is not the Bible, but our common needs, hurts, and interests as human beings. You cannot start with a text, expecting the unchurched to be fascinated by it. You must first capture their attention, and then move them to the truth of God's Word. By starting with a topic that interests the unchurched and then showing what the Bible says about it, you can grab their attention, disarm prejudices, and create an interest in the Bible that wasn't there before.[10]

---

[10] Rick Warren, *The Purpose Driven Church* (Grand Rapids, MI: Zondervan, 1995), 294–95.

But such a bait-and-switch approach is really just a recipe for compromise—tempting pastors to tickle the ears of their audience or water down the gospel in an effort to be more appealing. In essence, this approach says that God's Word is irrelevant and makes human ingenuity the key to interesting sinners in the gospel. It is therefore an approach that should be categorically rejected. As James Heidinger writes:

> Evangelical pastors and theologians can learn from the mainline experience of placing relevance above truth. We must avoid the lure of novelty and soft sell, which, we are told, will make it easier for moderns to believe. Methods may change, but never the message. . . . We are called to be faithful stewards of a great and reliable theological heritage. We have truths to affirm and errors to avoid. We must not try to make these truths more appealing or user friendly by watering them down. We must guard against a trendy "theological bungee-jumping" that merely entertains the watching crowd.[11]

We are called to preach the Bible consistently and accurately, fixed on the text as the revealed Word of God which, through the power of the Spirit, alone has the power to save and sanctify souls. When we do this, we can be confident that God is pleased, since our preaching will be in keeping with his Word (cf. 2 Tim. 2:15; 4:2).

9) Because God's Word Explained Ignites Interest in Personal Bible Study

Another motivation for biblical preaching is that when the pastor diligently studies and teaches God's Word, he demonstrates the value and blessing of personal Bible study before his congregation. People are dramatically impacted by the power of the Word

---

[11] James V. Heidinger II, "Toxic Pluralism," *Christianity Today* (April 5, 1993), 16–17.

through him. And when they see that the Word impacts them through their pastor, they are motivated to follow that model.

Over the last forty years, God has given me the privilege of studying and preaching his Word several times each week. Over these decades, my enthusiasm for the truth has only increased as I become more and more aware of the glory of the God of Scripture and his awesome works. The people in our churches will see such enthusiasm, because it will inevitably spill over in our preaching each Lord's Day. When they do, they will be prompted and encouraged in their own personal study throughout the week.

Expositional preaching also teaches people the principles of interpretation applicable to their personal Scripture study. As a Bible preacher, you are a living demonstration of hermeneutics. When you preach effectively, you take people through the process in the text that yields the true interpretation. You are training your people in a method of careful examination of the text, so that they can be like the Bereans who tested everything by a true understanding of the Word.

Show me a church where there is strong Bible teaching over an enduring period of time, and I will show you a congregation that is studying the Word of God on their own, skilled in the science of interpretation that has been modeled for them by their pastor. But show me a church where the Word of God is not taught in the pulpit, and I'll show you a place where biblical illiteracy, doctrinal confusion, and spiritual apathy at the personal level is rampant. The people will not rise to a level that is higher than their teacher. They will follow the example of their leaders. So, if we love God's Word, our people will too. If we don't, they won't either.

10) Because God's Word Builds a Ministry with a Divine Foundation

Finally, a ministry that centers on the preaching of God's Word is a ministry that is, by definition, wholly dependent on God. Rather than relying on gimmicks or ploys, it relies on God himself for both its content and direction.

Early in my ministry I committed before the Lord to worry only about the depth of my work, and I would let him take care of the breadth of it. Needless to say, he has extended it far beyond what I could have ever thought possible. But market appeal was not something I ever strategized about, as if trying to think of schemes for how to produce popularity or numerical growth. Instead, my focus was on teaching the Bible—deeply, consistently, and accurately. Beyond that, I determined simply to depend on the Lord.

When pastors preach God's message rather than one of their own invention, they demonstrate that they are fully depending on God for results. It is his Word that is taught; it is his Spirit who works; it is his power that convicts and transforms. We simply convey the message faithfully, and when people respond, God receives all of the glory.

That, ultimately, is why I continue to preach the Word after forty years of ministry. The goal of my life, from the outset, has been ministry faithfulness for the glory of Christ. That should be the aim of every pastor. What could be more glorifying to him than to exalt his message, bring it to bear in the lives of his people, and depend fully on him for the results? As Timothy was charged by Paul, so every pastor, if he is to be found faithful, must embrace his sacred calling:

> I solemnly charge you in the presence of God and of Christ Jesus, who is to judge the living and the dead, and by His appearing and His kingdom: preach the word; be ready in season and out of season; reprove, rebuke, exhort, with great patience and instruction. For the time will come when they will not endure sound doctrine; but wanting to have their ears tickled, they will accumulate for themselves teachers in accordance to their own desires, and will turn away their ears from the truth and will turn aside to myths. But you, be sober in all things, endure hardship, do the work of

an evangelist, fulfill your ministry. . . . I have fought the good fight, I have finished the course, I have kept the faith; in the future there is laid up for me the crown of righteousness, which the Lord, the righteous Judge, will award to me on that day; and not only to me, but also to all who have loved His appearing. . . . The Lord will rescue me from every evil deed, and will bring me safely to His heavenly kingdom; to Him be the glory forever and ever. Amen. (2 Tim. 4:1–5, 7–8, 18)

TOGETHER FOR THE GOSPEL AFFIRMATIONS AND DENIALS (2006)

We are brothers in Christ united in one great cause—to stand together for the Gospel. We are convinced that the Gospel of Jesus Christ has been misrepresented, misunderstood, and marginalized in many churches and among many who claim the name of Christ. Compromise of the Gospel has led to the preaching of false gospels, the seduction of many minds and movements, and the weakening of the church's Gospel witness.

As in previous moments of theological and spiritual crisis in the church, we believe that the answer to this confusion and compromise lies in a comprehensive recovery and reaffirmation of the Gospel—and in Christians banding together in Gospel churches that display God's glory in this fallen world.

We are also brothers united in deep concern for the church and the Gospel. This concern is specifically addressed to certain trends within the church today. We are concerned about the tendency of so many churches to substitute technique for truth, therapy for theology, and management for ministry.

We are also concerned that God's glorious purpose for Christ's church is often eclipsed in concern by so many other issues, programs, technologies, and priorities. Furthermore, confusion over crucial questions concerning the authority of the Bible, the meaning of the Gospel, and the nature of truth itself have gravely weakened the church in terms of its witness, its work, and its identity.

We stand together for the Gospel—and for a full and gladdening recovery of the Gospel in the church. We are convinced that such a recovery will be evident in the form of faithful Gospel churches, each bearing faithful witness to the glory of God and the power of the Gospel of Jesus Christ.

ARTICLE I

We affirm that the sole authority for the Church is the Bible, verbally inspired, inerrant, infallible, and totally suffcient and trustworthy.

We deny that the Bible is a mere witness to the divine revelation, or that any portion of Scripture is marked by error or the effects of human sinfulness.

ARTICLE II

We affirm that the authority and sufficiency of Scripture extends to the entire Bible, and therefore that the Bible is our final authority for all doctrine and practice.

We deny that any portion of the Bible is to be used in an effort to deny the truthfulness or trustworthiness of any other portion. We further deny any effort to identify a canon within the canon or, for example, to set the words of Jesus against the writings of Paul.

ARTICLE III

We affirm that truth ever remains a central issue for the Church, and that the church must resist the allure of pragmatism and postmodern conceptions of truth as substitutes for obedience to the comprehensive truth claims of Scripture.

We deny that truth is merely a product of social construction or that the truth of the Gospel can be expressed or grounded in anything less than total confidence in the veracity of the Bible, the historicity of biblical events, and the ability of language to convey understandable truth in sentence form. We further deny that the church can establish its ministry on a foundation of pragmatism, current marketing techniques, or contemporary cultural fashions.

ARTICLE IV

We affirm the centrality of expository preaching in the church and the urgent need for a recovery of biblical exposition and the public reading of Scripture in worship.

We deny that God-honoring worship can marginalize or neglect the ministry of the Word as manifested through exposition and public reading. We further deny that a church devoid of true biblical preaching can survive as a Gospel church.

ARTICLE V

We affirm that the Bible reveals God to be infinite in all his perfections, and thus truly omniscient, omnipotent, timeless, and self-existent. We further affirm that God possesses perfect knowledge of all things, past, present, and future, including all human thoughts, acts, and decisions.

We deny that the God of the Bible is in any way limited in terms of knowledge or power or any other perfection or attribute, or that God has in any way limited his own perfections.

ARTICLE VI

We affirm that the doctrine of the Trinity is a Christian essential, bearing witness to the ontological reality of the one true God in three divine persons, Father, Son, and Holy Spirit, each of the same substance and perfections.

We deny the claim that the Trinity is not an essential doctrine, or that the Trinity can be understood in merely economic or functional categories.

ARTICLE VII

We affirm that Jesus Christ is true God and true Man, in perfect, undiluted, and unconfused union throughout his incarnation and now eternally. We also affirm that Christ died on the cross as a substitute for sinners, as a sacrifice for sin, and as a propitiation of the wrath of God toward sinners. We affirm the death, burial, and bodily resurrection of Christ as essential to the Gospel. We further affirm that Jesus Christ is Lord over His church, and that Christ will reign over the entire cosmos in fulfillment of the Father's gracious purpose.

We deny that the substitutionary character of Christ's atonement for sin can be compromised without serious injury to the Gospel or denied without repudiating the Gospel. We further deny that Jesus Christ is visible only in weakness, rather than in power, Lordship, or royal reign, or, conversely, that Christ is visible only in power, and never in weakness.

ARTICLE VIII

We affirm that salvation is all of grace, and that the Gospel is revealed to us in doctrines that most faithfully exalt God's sovereign purpose to save sinners and in His determination to save his redeemed people by grace alone, through faith alone, in Christ alone, to His glory alone.

We deny that any teaching, theological system, or means of presenting the Gospel that denies the centrality of God's grace as His gift of unmerited favor to sinners in Christ can be considered true doctrine.

ARTICLE IX

We affirm that the Gospel of Jesus Christ is God's means of bringing salvation to His people, that sinners are commanded to believe the Gospel, and that the church is commissioned to preach and teach the Gospel to all nations.

We deny that evangelism can be reduced to any program, technique, or marketing approach. We further deny that salvation can be separated from repentance toward God and faith in our Lord Jesus Christ.

ARTICLE X

We affirm that salvation comes to those who truly believe and confess that Jesus Christ is Lord.

We deny that there is salvation in any other name, or that saving faith can take any form other than conscious belief in the Lord Jesus Christ and His saving acts.

ARTICLE XI

We affirm the continuity of God's saving purpose and the Christological unity of the covenants. We further affirm a basic distinction between law and grace, and that the true Gospel exalts Christ's atoning work as the consummate and perfect fulfillment of the law.

We deny that the Bible presents any other means of salvation than God's gracious acceptance of sinners in Christ.

ARTICLE XII

We affirm that sinners are justified only through faith in Christ, and that justification by faith alone is both essential and central to the Gospel.

We deny that any teaching that minimizes, denies, or confuses justification by faith alone can be considered true to the Gospel. We further deny that any teaching that separates regeneration and faith is a true rendering of the Gospel.

ARTICLE XIII

We affirm that the righteousness of Christ is imputed to believers by God's decree alone, and that this righteousness, imputed to the believer through faith alone, is the only righteousness that justifies.

We deny that such righteousness is earned or deserved in any manner, is infused within the believer to any degree, or is realized in the believer through anything other than faith alone.

ARTICLE XIV

We affirm that the shape of Christian discipleship is congregational, and that God's purpose is evident in faithful Gospel congregations, each displaying God's glory in the marks of authentic ecclesiology.

We deny that any Christian can truly be a faithful disciple apart from the teaching, discipline, fellowship, and accountability of a congregation of fellow disciples, organized as a Gospel church. We further deny that the Lord's Supper can faithfully be administered apart from the right practice of church discipline.

ARTICLE XV

We affirm that evangelical congregations are to work together in humble and voluntary cooperation and that the spiritual fellowship of Gospel congregations bears witness to the unity of the Church and the glory of God.

We deny that loyalty to any denomination or fellowship of churches can take precedence over the claims of truth and faithfulness to the Gospel.

ARTICLE XVI

We affirm that the Scripture reveals a pattern of complementary order between men and women, and that this order is itself a testimony to the Gospel, even as it is the gift of our Creator and Redeemer. We also affirm that all Christians are called to service within the body of Christ, and that God has given to both men and women important and strategic roles within the home, the church, and the society. We further affirm that the teaching office of the church is assigned only to those men who are called of God in fulfillment of the biblical teachings and that men are to lead in their homes as husbands and fathers who fear and love God.

We deny that the distinction of roles between men and women revealed in the Bible is evidence of mere cultural conditioning or a manifestation of male oppression or prejudice against women. We also deny that this biblical distinction of roles excludes women from meaningful ministry in Christ's kingdom. We further deny that any church can confuse these issues without damaging its witness to the Gospel.

ARTICLE XVII

We affirm that God calls his people to display his glory in the reconciliation of the nations within the Church, and that God's pleasure in this reconciliation is evident in the gathering of believers from every tongue and tribe and people and nation. We acknowledge that the staggering magnitude of injustice against African-Americans in the name of the Gospel presents a special opportunity for displaying the repentance, forgiveness, and restoration promised in the Gospel. We further affirm that evangelical Christianity in America bears a unique responsibility to demonstrate this reconciliation with our African-American brothers and sisters.

We deny that any church can accept racial prejudice, discrimination, or division without betraying the Gospel.

ARTICLE XVIII

We affirm that our only sure and confident hope is in the sure and certain promises of God. Thus, our hope is an eschatological hope, grounded in our confidence that God will bring all things to consummation in a manner that will bring greatest glory to his own name, greatest preeminence to his Son, and greatest joy for his redeemed people.

We deny that we are to find ultimate fulfillment or happiness in this world, or that God's ultimate purpose is for us to find merely a more meaningful and fulfilling life in this fallen world. We further deny that any teaching that offers health and wealth as God's assured promises in this life can be considered a true gospel.

> *Now I would remind you, brothers, of the gospel I preached to you,*
> *which you received, in which you stand, and by which*
> *you are being saved, if you hold fast to the word*
> *I preached to you—unless you believed in vain.*
> *For I delivered to you as of first importance what I also received:*
> *that Christ died for our sins in accordance with the*
> *Scriptures, that he was buried, that he was raised*
> *on the third day in accordance with the Scriptures . . .*
>
> 1 CORINTHIANS 15:1–4

> *Then I saw another angel flying directly overhead,*
> *with an eternal gospel to proclaim to those who dwell*
> *on earth, to every nation and tribe and language and people.*
> *And he said with a loud voice, "Fear God and give him glory,*
> *because the hour of his judgment has come, and worship*
> *him who made heaven and earth, the sea and the springs of water."*
>
> REVELATION 14:6–7

Mark E. Dever

J. Ligon Duncan III

C. J. Mahaney

R. Albert Mohler, Jr.

GENERAL INDEX

SCRIPTURE INDEX